Introduction to Chemistry for Biology Students

Third Edition

George I. Sackheim

Science Instructor,
St. Francis Hospital
School of Nursing,
Evanston, Illinois

Associate Professor Emeritus, Chemistry,
University of Illinois at Chicago

formerly Coordinator of Biological
and Physical Sciences,
Michael Reese Hospital
and Medical Center, Chicago

EMI EDUCATIONAL METHODS/CHICAGO
A DIVISION OF DEVELOPMENT SYSTEMS CORPORATION

Library of Congress Catalog Card Number 65-22496

ISBN 0-88462-016-6

EDUCATIONAL METHODS/Chicago,
a subsidiary company of Longman Group Limited.

84 85 10 9 8 7 6 5 4 3 2

Contents

To the Student

This book is part of the EMI Programed Biology Studies, a series that approaches biology at its most fundamental level. The basic questions it raises and explores are among the most critical and exciting issues science must face in the years ahead: What are the basic chemical processes underlying the important biological phenomena? What are the essential differences between living and nonliving matter? What are the conditions under which molecules organize into living matter? Can these conditions be duplicated experimentally?

Introduction to Chemistry is not an ordinary book. It has been programed to help you review or learn quickly and efficiently the basic facts, concepts, and terminology of chemistry that are essential to an understanding of biological phenomena. Most modern biology courses and textbooks place increasing emphasis on the chemical processes that underlie the critical biological functions.

If you have already had a course in basic chemistry, this programed book will serve as an effective review of the fundamental concepts. If you have had no previous chemistry, the program will give you the background you need to gain a clear understanding of the biological processes you will be studying.

Do not try to skip around in this book. Start at the beginning and proceed through it at the pace most comfortable for you. Under no circumstances should you rush through the program. Whether it takes you two hours or six to complete the program is of little importance. Your primary objective should be to master the material in the program no matter how long that may take.

The material covered in this book will be of most help to you if you complete it during the first two weeks of your biology course. If you follow that schedule, you will be ready for and able to handle the chemical aspects of biology when they begin to appear in the course.

Once you have completed the program you may want to review certain material. To simplify this process, the book contains a detailed table of contents which you will find a useful index for locating specific topics. If you follow the directions and complete this program, you will learn to:

- recognize elements present in various compounds;

- know what is meant by pH and by ionization;

- recognize acids, bases, and salts;

- discriminate between electrolytes and non-electrolytes;

- understand oxidation and reduction;

- know what isotopes are;

- recognize various organic functional groups;

- differentiate between carbohydrates, fats, and proteins.

George I. Sackheim

How to Use This Book

This may be a new type of instructional book for many of you. Its subject matter has been broken down into a series of numbered frames. Each builds on information you have learned in preceding frames. For that reason it is important that you do not skip around in the program. The sequence of the frames is important and is designed to help you learn more efficiently.

Respond at Every Frame

Some frames present new information; others review material presented earlier. Almost every frame presents a learning task which requires some response from you. You may be asked to make any one of the following types of responses:

● writing an answer in a blank space;

● labelling a diagram;

● drawing a simple diagram;

● selecting the correct answer from among several alternatives;

● writing a sentence in answer to a question.

Once you have written or marked your answer you'll want to find out whether or not you were right. Programed instruction provides you with important feedback by giving you the answers to the questions asked. The answers are separated from each question by a single line. *Do not look at the correct answer until after you have marked your own answer.* If you look before answering, you will only impair your own learning.

Use an Answer Mask

To avoid seeing the correct answer inadvertently before recording your own answer, take a blank piece of 8½" x 11" paper, fold it in half, and use it as an Answer Mask.

Here is how you use it.

1. As you start a page, cover it with the Answer Mask.
2. Slide the mask down until you see the horizontal line across the entire page. This line separates each frame from its correct answer.
3. When you reach the horizontal line, stop moving the mask. Read the frame carefully; then, record your answer. Make sure you write each answer, or do whatever the directions ask. Do *not* simply think the answer and then go on. Actually writing or marking your answer is part of learning.
4. Slide the mask down to reveal the correct answer.
5. If your answer was correct, move the mask down to the next heavy horizontal line and proceed with the new frame.
6. If your answer was wrong, reread the frame (if necessary, reread several frames) until you understand your error and know why the answer given is correct. Then go on.

Review Questions

At the end of almost every chapter you will find a short review section. Answer all the questions in this section before looking at the correct answers. These quizzes not only help you review and reinforce what you have learned; they also give you a way to evaluate your own chapter-by-chapter progress through the program.

This program also has a separate final examination covering all the material in the program. Your instructor may ask you to take that exam after you have completed the program. If you are using the program for independent study, you may find it valuable to take the final exam to check on your own learning achievement.

I
ATOMIC STRUCTURE

1.   Atoms are made up of several components. Collectively these components are called the *elementary particles.*

We will be discussing the three major elementary particles: *protons, neutrons,* and *electrons.*

Here is a diagram of an atom:

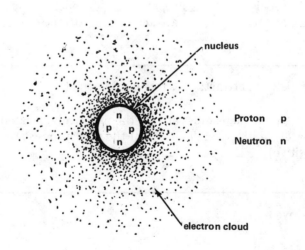

nucleus

Proton   p

Neutron   n

electron cloud

The protons (p) and the neutrons (n) are packed together in an inner core called the _nucleus_. The outer part of the atom contains electrons. This outer part of the atom is called the _electron cloud_.

---

nucleus; electron cloud

2. The electron cloud has a negative electrical charge. What type of charge would you expect the electron to have?

negative

---

a negative electrical charge, since the electron cloud consists of electrons

3. The electron has a *negative electrical charge,* and is symbolized by e-. Remember that *like* electrical charges repel each other, and *unlike* charges attract.

Indicate whether the following pairs of charges would attract or repel each other. (Check the correct word for each pair.)

a. (+) (+)   b. (-) (+)   c. (-) (-)   d. (+) (-)
___✓___ repel   _____ repel   ___✓___ repel   _____ repel
_____ attract   ___✓___ attract   _____ attract   ___✓___ attract

---

a. repel; b. attract; c. repel; d. attract

4. The nucleus must attract the negatively charged electrons. Therefore, the overall charge of the nucleus must be (negative/positive) _positive_.

---

positive

2

5. The neutron was named for its electrical characteristics. It has no electrical charge; it is neutral.

This means that the positive charge of the nucleus must be due to the *second type of particle* it contains. This second type of particle is the _proton_ .

---

proton

6. So far, then, we have this picture of atomic structure:

a. An atom consists of an inner part, or _nucleus_ , that is made up of _neutrons_ and _protons_ .
b. The electron has what type of charge? _negative_
c. The proton has what type of charge? _positive_
d. The neutron has a charge of _~~neutral~~ zero_

---

a. nucleus, protons, and neutrons; b. negative;
c. positive; d. zero (0)

7. The charge on the electron balances the charge on the proton. If the electron has a charge of −1, then the proton would have a charge of: (check one)

_____−1   _✓_+1   _____±1

+1

8. An atom with one proton in its nucleus and one electron outside that nucleus would therefore have an overall charge of (+1, −1, 0) _0_ .

3

9. Normally, atoms are electrically neutral. This means that a normal atom will contain: (check one)

    _____ a.   more protons than electrons
    _____ b.   more electrons than protons
    __✓__ c.   an equal number of protons and electrons

---

c.   an equal number of protons and electrons

10. An atom with 12 protons in the nucleus would have how many electrons around the nucleus? __12__

12

11. The atom with the simplest atomic structure is hydrogen.

The nucleus of the hydrogen atom consists of one __proton__.

HYDROGEN ATOM

The outer part of the atom, the electron cloud, contains one __electron__.

(For simplicity we shall merely indicate the electron(s) outside the nucleus, and omit the electron cloud.)

---

proton; electron

12.

HELIUM ATOM

The helium atom is a little more complicated.

It contains: (how many?)

_____2_____ neutrons
_____2_____ protons
_____2_____ electrons

2; 2; 2

13. There are approximately 100 known elements. Each element has two numbers associated with it—numbers that give certain facts about the structure of its atoms.

The first number is the *atomic number.* This is the number of protons in the nucleus of the atom. Hydrogen, the simplest atom, contains only one proton, so the atomic number of hydrogen is _____1_____.

1

14. Uranium is the most complicated of the elements that occur naturally. A uranium atom contains 92 protons, 146 neutrons, and 92 electrons.

The atomic number of uranium is _____92_____.

92

15. An atom of carbon, atomic number 12, must have a nucleus containing _____12_____ protons.

If the nucleus contains 12 protons, there must be how many electrons? _12_

12; 12

16. Therefore, the atomic number of an element indicates the number of _protons_ in the nucleus of the atom, and also the number of _electrons_ outside the nucleus.

---

protons; electrons

17. The second number associated with each atom is the *mass number*. The mass number expresses the sum of the masses of the particles in the atom.

A proton has a mass of 1 atomic mass unit. An electron is considered to have zero mass, or a mass of 0.

Thus, a hydrogen atom has a mass of _1_. (If you don't know, see frame 11.)

1

18. The helium atom has a mass number of 4.

a. The 2 protons in the helium atom have a total of how many atomic mass units? _2_
b. The 2 electrons in the helium atom have a total of how many atomic mass units? _0_

c. Therefore, for the helium atom to have a mass number of 4, the 2 neutrons must contain how many atomic mass units? __2__
d. If 2 neutrons contain 2 atomic mass units, a neutron must have an atomic mass of __1__.

---

a. 2; b. 0; c. 2; d. 1

19. Since the electrons, which have practically no mass, are located outside the nucleus, the entire mass of the atom can be considered to be located:

_____ ✓ a.   in its electron cloud
_____ ✓ b.   in the nucleus

---

b. in the nucleus

20. The *atomic number* indicates the number of protons (each with atomic mass 1) inside the nucleus of an atom.

The mass number indicates the number of protons and neutrons (each with atomic mass 1) in the nucleus.

Therefore, the number of neutrons can be determined by subtracting the atomic number from the mass number.

The sodium atom has a mass number of 23 and an atomic number of 11. The number of neutrons in the nucleus of the sodium atom is __12__.

12

21. The carbon atom has an atomic number of 6 and a mass number of 12. The carbon atom contains: (how many?)

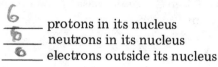

_6_ protons in its nucleus
_6_ neutrons in its nucleus
_6_ electrons outside its nucleus

6; 6; 6

22. The element phosphorus has an atomic number of 15 and a mass number of 31. Indicate on the blank lines on the diagram the number of protons, neutrons, and electrons.

PHOSPHORUS ATOM

PHOSPHORUS ATOM

23. Diagram the structure of the magnesium atom, atomic number 12 and mass number 24.

MAGNESIUM ATOM

MAGNESIUM ATOM

8

24. The uranium atom has the atomic structure shown here:

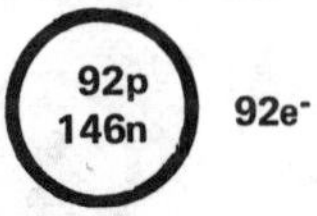

URANIUM ATOM

Therefore, the uranium atom has an atomic number of __92__ and a mass number of __238__.

92; 238

Isotopes

25. Draw the structure of a carbon atom, atomic number 6 and mass number 12.

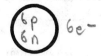

Now draw the structure of a carbon atom, atomic number 6 and mass number 13.

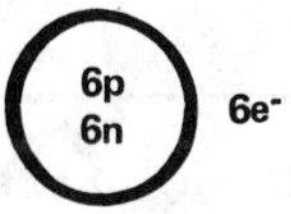

CARBON—12

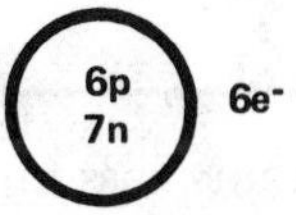

CARBON—13

26. Here are the structures you drew for the two carbon atoms:

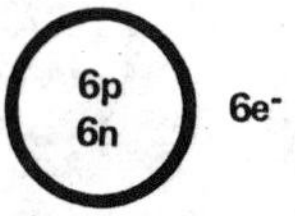

CARBON−12 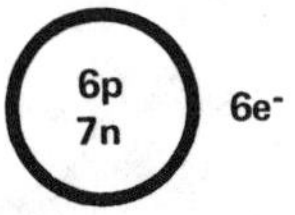   CARBON−13

a.   These atoms have: (check one)

_____✓_____ the same atomic number
_____ different atomic numbers

b.   These atoms have: (check one)

_____ the same mass number
_____✓_____ different mass numbers

Such atoms are called *isotopes.*

---

a.   the same atomic number; b.   different mass numbers

27. Isotopes, then, may be defined as atoms that have:

_____ a. the same atomic number and the same mass
            number
_____ b. different atomic numbers
_____✓_____ c. different mass numbers and the same atomic
            number

---

c.   different mass numbers and the same atomic number

28. Draw the two isotopes of chlorine, atomic number 17 and mass numbers 35 and 37.

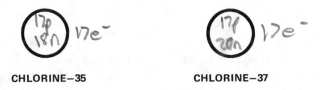

CHLORINE—35 CHLORINE—37

CHLORINE—35 CHLORINE—37

29. Draw the three isotopes of hydrogen, atomic number 1 and mass numbers 1, 2, and 3.

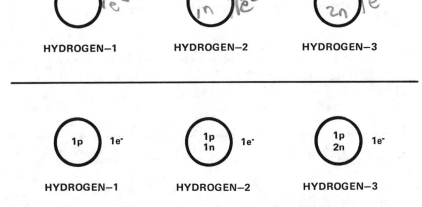

HYDROGEN—1 HYDROGEN—2 HYDROGEN—3

HYDROGEN—1 HYDROGEN—2 HYDROGEN—3

Electron Energy Levels

30. The electrons are located outside of the nucleus of the atom. These electrons make up the electron cloud, which may be subdivided into different energy levels.

The first energy level is nearest the nucleus; then comes the second energy level, the third energy level, and so on.

31. Each energy level can hold a certain maximum number of electrons. This maximum number may be determined by using the formula $X = 2n^2$ (X is the maximum number of electrons in energy level number n).

Using the formula $X = 2n^2$, if n = 1, then X = _2_. The energy level indicated by n = 1 is the first energy level. Therefore, the first energy level can hold a maximum of _2_ electrons.

2; 2

32. Can the first energy level hold fewer than two electrons? _Yes_ Can the first energy level hold more than two electrons? _no_

---

yes; no

33. For the second energy level, where n = 2, the maximum number of electrons is _8_ .

8

34. The maximum number of electrons in the third energy level
is __16__. The maximum number of electrons in the fourth energy
level is __32__ .

18; 32

35. Label the maximum number of electrons possible in each
energy level in the diagram.

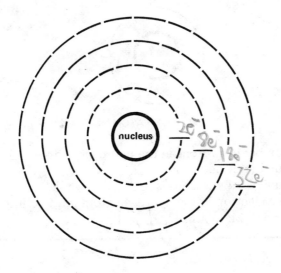

---

2 e⁻ in the first energy level; 8 e⁻ in the second energy level; 18 e⁻
in the third energy level; 32 e⁻ in the fourth energy level

36. The following rules must be observed when considering the placement of electrons in the various energy levels.

The first energy level must be filled with 2 electrons before electrons can go into the second energy level.

The second energy level must be filled with __8__ electrons before electrons can go into the third energy level.

8

37. On the diagram, show the structure of the hydrogen atom, atomic number 1, mass number 1.

HYDROGEN ATOM

a.   The number of protons in the hydrogen atom is __1__.
b.   The number of neutrons is __0__.
c.   The number of electrons is __1__.
d.   The one electron in the hydrogen atom must go into which energy level—1st, 2nd, or 3rd?__1st__.

---

a. 1; b. 0; c. 1; d. 1st

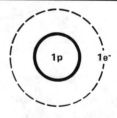

HYDROGEN ATOM

38. In the space provided, draw the structure of the helium atom, atomic number 2 and mass number 4.

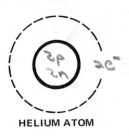

HELIUM ATOM

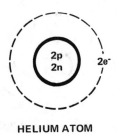

HELIUM ATOM

39. Now let's look at the structure for the lithium atom, atomic number 3 and mass number 7.

a.   The number of protons in the lithium atom is ___3___.
b.   The number of neutrons in the lithium atom is ___4___.
c.   The number of electrons in the lithium atom is ___3___.

---

  a. 3;   b. 4;   c. 3

40. There are 3 electrons in the lithium atom. How many energy levels will the lithium atom have? ___2___
(If you aren't sure, check frame 36).

Complete the diagram of the lithium atom.

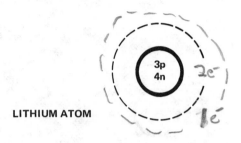

LITHIUM ATOM

$3p$
$4n$

$2e^-$

$1e^-$

2

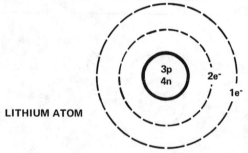

LITHIUM ATOM

$3p$
$4n$

$2e^-$

$1e^-$

41. The carbon atom has atomic number 6 and mass number 12.

The carbon atom contains __6__ protons.
The carbon atom contains __6__ neutrons.
The carbon atom contains __6__ electrons.

Complete the structure of the carbon atom.

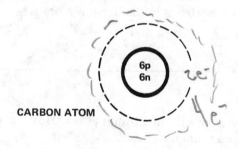

CARBON ATOM

$6p$
$6n$

$2e^-$

$4e^-$

6; 6; 6

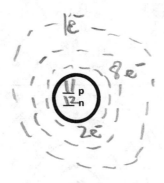

6p
6n   2e⁻
              4e⁻

CARBON ATOM

42. a. In the element sodium, atomic number 11, there are how many electrons? __11__

b. How many energy levels will the sodium atom have?__3__

c. How many electrons will each energy level of the sodium atom have?

1st energy level __2__
2nd energy level __8__
3rd energy level __1__

Diagram the complete structure of the sodium atom, atomic number 11 and mass number 23.

1e⁻

8e⁻

11p
12n

2e⁻

---

a. 11;   b. 3;   c. 2, 8, 1

Structure of sodium atom shown on next page.

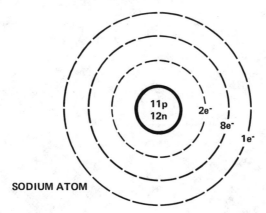

SODIUM ATOM

43. Diagram the structure of the silicon atom, atomic number 14 and mass number 28.

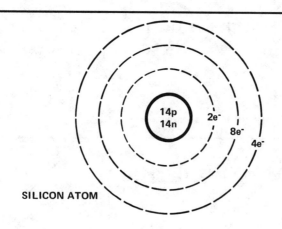

SILICON ATOM

Chemical Symbols

44. Each of the approximately 100 elements has its own name and its own properties. The symbol for an element is usually an abbreviation for its name. Frequently the abbreviation is merely the first letter of that name. The following table lists some of these elements.

Element	Symbol
hydrogen	H
carbon	C
oxygen	O
nitrogen	N
phosphorus	P
sulfur	S

45. What elements are present in the compound CO_2? _Carbon Oxygen_ .

---

carbon and oxygen

46. What elements are present in ammonia, NH_3? _Nitrogen hydrogen_ .

---

nitrogen and hydrogen

47. What elements are present in glucose, $C_6H_{12}O_6$? _Carbon hydrogen, and oxygen_ .

carbon, hydrogen, and oxygen

48. What elements does the compound $C_6H_7NSO_3$ contain?
Carbon, hydrogen, nitrogen, oxygen, and sulfur.

carbon, hydrogen, nitrogen, sulfur, and oxygen

49. When the names of more than one element begin with the same letter, frequently the second letter of the name is added to the symbol. Note that only the first letter of the symbol is capitalized.

Here are some of the elements whose symbols are the first two letters of their names. Write the symbols for each.

Element	Symbol
calcium	Ca
bromine	Br
silicon	Si
barium	Ba

Ca; Br; Si; Ba

50. The compound $CaBr_2$ contains the elements calcium
and bromine.

calcium, bromine

51. The compound BaO_2 contains the elements _Barium_ and _Oxygen_.

---

barium, oxygen

52. The compound CaC_2O_4 contains the elements _Calcium_ _Carbon_ _Oxygen_.

---

calcium, carbon, and oxygen

53. A molecule of sucrose contains 12 atoms of carbon, 22 atoms of hydrogen, and 11 atoms of oxygen. The formula for sucrose is _$C_{12}H_{22}O_{11}$_.

$C_{12}H_{22}O_{11}$

54. A molecule of calcium sulfate contains 1 atom of calcium, 1 atom of sulfur, and 4 atoms of oxygen. The formula for calcium sulfate is _$CaSO_4$_.

$CaSO_4$

55. There are several elements whose symbols are not derived from the first letter or first two letters of their English names. Some of those elements are listed in the table at the top of the next page.

Element	Symbol
chlorine	Cl
sodium	Na (from the Latin *natrium*)
magnesium	Mg
potassium	K (from the Latin *kalium*)
zinc	Zn
iron	Fe (from the Latin *ferrum*)

Write the name of the element represented by each of the symbols below:

H _Hydrogen_   C _Carbon_

N _Nitrogen_   S _Sulfur_

O _oxygen_   Si _Silicon_

Ca _Calcium_   Br _Bromine_

Na _Sodium_   Zn _Zinc_

K _potassivm_   Fe _Iron_

Hydrogen	Carbon
Nitrogen	Sulfur
Oxygen	*Silicon*
Calcium	*Bromine*
sodium	*Zinc*
potassium	iron

56. What elements are present in each of the following compounds?

a. KBr _Potassium Bromine_

b. CCl_4 _Carbon chlorine_

22

c. NaOH _Sodium Oxygen Hydrogen_
d. $MgCl_2$ _Magnesium Chlorine_
e. $NaNO_3$ _Sodium Nitrogen Oxygen_
f. $K_3FeC_6N_6$ _Potassium, Iron, carbon, Nitrogen_

---

a. potassium and bromine;
b. carbon and chlorine;
c. sodium, oxygen, and hydrogen;
d. magnesium and chlorine;
e. sodium, nitrogen, and oxygen;
f. potassium, iron, carbon, and nitrogen.

57. One molecule of vitamin B_{12} contains:

> 63 atoms of carbon
> 90 atoms of hydrogen
> 14 atoms of oxygen
> 14 atoms of nitrogen
> 1 atom of phosphorus
> 1 atom of cobalt (Co)

The formula for vitamin B_{12} is _$C_{63}H_{90}O_{14}N_{14}PCo$_.

$C_{63}H_{90}O_{14}N_{14}PCo$

58. A molecule of biotin, one of the B vitamins, contains:

> 10 atoms of carbon
> 16 atoms of hydrogen
> 3 atoms of oxygen
> 2 atoms of nitrogen
> 1 atom of sulfur

The formula for biotin is _$C_{10}H_{16}O_3N_2S$_.

$C_{10}H_{16}O_3N_2S$

59. Heme, a constituent of hemoglobin, contains:

> 34 atoms of carbon
> 35 atoms of hydrogen
> 4 atoms of nitrogen
> 4 atoms of oxygen
> 1 atom of iron

The formula for heme is $C_{34}H_{35}N_4O_4Fe$.

$C_{34}H_{35}N_4O_4Fe$

60. Chlorophyll has the formula $C_{55}H_{68}O_5N_4Mg$. It contains the elements:

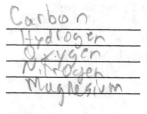

Carbon
Hydrogen
Oxygen
Nitrogen
Magnesium

---

carbon, hydrogen, oxygen, nitrogen, magnesium

II

IONIZATION

Atoms and Molecules

61. Atoms combine to form *molecules*. A molecule contains two or more atoms.

The molecule O_2 contains how many atoms of oxygen? _____ 2

2

62. Each molecule of glucose, $C_6H_{12}O_6$, contains:

_____ 6 _____ atoms of carbon
_____ 12 _____ atoms of hydrogen
_____ 6 _____ atoms of oxygen

6, 12, 6

63. The *1* for one atom of an element is understood, and not written in the formula. Each molecule of carbon dioxide, CO_2, contains 1 atom of carbon and (how many?) _____ 2 _____ atoms of oxygen.

2

64. A water molecule is composed of two hydrogen atoms and one oxygen atom.

Write the formula for a water molecule. _H₂O_

H_2O

65. When you want to represent more than one molecule of a compound, the number of molecules precedes the symbols. Thus, $6CO_2$ indicates how many molecules of carbon dioxide? _6_

How would eight molecules of water be represented? _8H₂O_

$6;\ 8H_2O$

66. The symbol H indicates: (check one)

_____ 1 molecule of hydrogen
__✓__ 1 atom of hydrogen

---

1 atom of hydrogen

67. The formula H_2 indicates one _molecule_ of _Hydrogen_, composed of how many atoms?

---

molecule, hydrogen; 2

26

68. The formula 2H$_2$ indicates ___2 molecules___ of hydro-gen.

---

two molecules

69. What do the following represent?

3O ___3 atoms of oxygen___

4N$_2$ ___4 molecules of Nitrogen___

7H$_2$O ___7 molecules of water___

---

3 atoms of oxygen; 4 molecules of nitrogen; 7 molecules of water

Ions and Ionic Bonds

70. Atoms contain equal numbers of protons and electrons. Thus, atoms are:

_____ a.   electropositive
_____ b.   electronegative
___✓___ c.   electrically neutral

---

c.   electrically neutral

71. The electron is a (negatively/positively) _negatively_ charged particle. So, if an atom loses an electron it will then have an overall (negative/positive) _positive_ charge.

---

negatively; positive

72. If an atom were to *gain* an extra electron, it would then have an overall _negative_ charge.

---

negative

73. An *ion* is an atom that has acquired an electrical charge by either losing or gaining an _electron_.

---

electron

74. Note that electrons, which are located outside the nucleus, are lost or gained in the formation of ions. The nucleus, which contains protons and neutrons, does not take part in the formation of ions.

If a hydrogen atom loses its electron, it becomes a hydrogen ion. Since it loses an electron, it is a (negatively/positively) _positively_ charged ion.

---

positively

75. Any atom that has lost or gained an electron is an ___*ion*___.

a. If an atom gains an electron, it becomes a ___*negatively*___ charged ion.
b. If an atom loses an electron, it becomes a ___*positively*___ charged ion.

---

ion;   a. negatively;   b. positively

76. Most atoms reach their most stable state when they have 8 electrons in their outer energy level, called the *valence shell.*

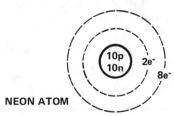

NEON ATOM

This atom of neon, for example, contains 10 electrons. Two of the electrons fill the first energy level, and the remaining 8 electrons are in the second energy level. So the second energy level of neon would be called its ___*valence shell.*___

---

valence shell

77. Neon has a completed outer energy level, one that can hold no more electrons. Thus, neon is a very (stable/unstable) ___*stable*___ atom. Such elements are usually unreactive.

---

stable

78. Look at this atom of chlorine.

CHLORINE ATOM

In chlorine, the outer energy level, or _valence shell_ , is the
_____third_____ energy level. It contains 7 electrons. Thus,
to attain a stable state the chlorine atom needs to gain how many
electrons? __1__

What is the symbol for chlorine? __Cl__

---

valence shell, third; 1; Cl

79. Suppose that an atom of chlorine does gain the one electron
it needs to become stable. Since it has gained an electron, it is
now a charged atom, called an __ion__.

Would it have a positive or negative charge? __negative__

---

ion; negative

80. Which of these symbols stands for the chloride ion (a chlorine atom that has gained one electron)? (Cl, Cl^+, Cl^-)__Cl^-__

Cl^-

30

81. If a chlorine atom is to gain an electron, some other atom must lose the electron. That atom could be sodium, the symbol for which is N̶a̶ ~~____~~.

The sodium atom has how many electrons in its outer energy level? 1

SODIUM ATOM

To become stable it will have to:

____ gain one electron
✓ lose one electron

Na; 1; lose one electron

82. When the sodium atom loses one electron it becomes a (positively/negatively) _positively_ charged _ion_.

---

positively, ion

83. Which symbol (Na, Na^+, or Na^-) should we use for the sodium ion? Na^+

Na^+

84. Positive and negative charges are indicated by raised plus (positive) or minus (negative) signs, respectively, with the number 1 being understood. Charges greater than 1 are written as raised numbers, with the number preceding the plus or minus sign.

Thus, Na^+ indicates a sodium ion with a charge of __+1__, Cl^- indicates a chloride ion with a charge of __-1__, and Mg^{2+} indicates a magnesium ion with a charge of __2__.

+1, -1, +2

85. How would an aluminum ion with a charge of +3 be indicated? __Al³⁺__ How would a sulfide ion with a charge of -2 be indicated? __S²⁻__

Al^{3+}; S^{2-}

86. $Na + Cl \longrightarrow Na^+ + Cl^-$
             (Reaction of sodium and chlorine)
    When a sodium atom reacts with a chlorine atom, the sodium atom (gains/loses) __loses__ one electron to form a sodium ion with a __positive__ charge of (how many?) __1__.

At the same time, the chlorine atom (gains/loses) __gains__ one electron to form an ion with a __negative__ charge of (how many?) __1__.

---

loses, positive, 1; gains, negative, 1

87. Look at this atom of magnesium. Its symbol is _Mg_ .

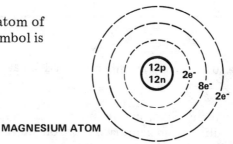

MAGNESIUM ATOM

It has ___2___ electrons in its outer energy level. So to gain stability, it will have to (gain/lose) ___lose___ (how many?) ___2___ electrons.

The symbol for the magnesium ion is (Mg^{2-}, Mg, Mg^{2+}) ___Mg^{2+}___ .

Mg; 2, lose, 2; Mg^{2+}

88. The reaction between magnesium and chlorine may be written as:

$$Mg + Cl_2 \longrightarrow Mg^{2+} + 2Cl^-$$

This reaction shows that one chlorine molecule reacts with one magnesium atom to form two chloride ions, each with a charge of ___−1___ , and one magnesium ion with a charge of ___+2___ .

-1, +2

89. The hydrogen atom, atomic number 1, has ___1___ electron(s) in its outer energy level.

90. The sulfur atom, atomic number 16, has how many energy levels? __3__

a.   How many electrons are in its outer energy level? __6__
b.   If a sulfur atom gains two electrons to fill its outer energy level, it will have a charge of __-2__.
c.   The symbol for the sulfide ion is __S²⁻__.

3; a. 6; b. -2; c. S^{2-}

91. How can we tell whether an atom will lose or gain electrons to reach a stable structure of eight electrons in its outer energy level?
Look over the diagrams here and on the top of the next page.

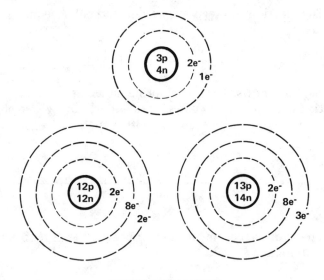

FORM POSITIVE IONS

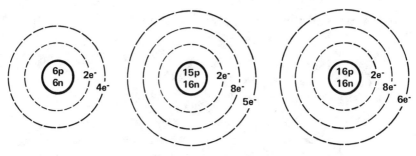

DO NOT FORM POSITIVE IONS

In general, an atom with (how many?) 1, 2, 3 electrons in its outer energy level tends to lose electrons and form a (positively/negatively) positively charged ion.

1, 2, or 3 (or equivalent answer); positively

92. Sodium has atomic number 11. How many electron(s) does it have in its outer energy level? 1

The sodium ion, therefore, is formed by the (loss/gain) loss of one electron.

The symbol for the sodium ion is Na+.

1; loss; Na+

35

93. Here is an aluminum atom:

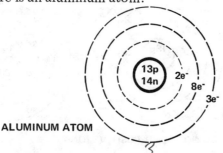

ALUMINUM ATOM

Its outer energy level contains ___3___ electrons. The aluminum ion is formed by the (loss/gain) ___loss___ of 3 electrons.

The symbol for the aluminum ion is ___Al^{3+}___.

3; loss; Al^{3+}

94. Magnesium, atomic number 12, forms a magnesium ion that may be represented as ___Mg^{2+}___.

Mg^{2+}

95. Look at these diagrams carefully.

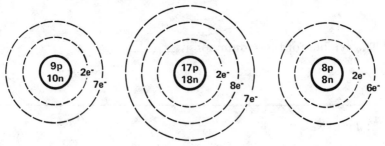

FORM NEGATIVE IONS

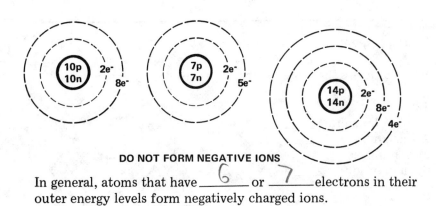

DO NOT FORM NEGATIVE IONS

In general, atoms that have ___6___ or ___7___ electrons in their outer energy levels form negatively charged ions.

---

6 or 7

96. When an atom gains electrons to fill its outer energy level, it forms ___negatively___ charged ions.

---

negatively

97. Fill in the following table for the fluorine (F) atom:

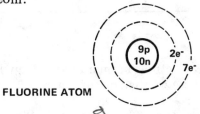

FLUORINE ATOM

Atomic number: ___9___
Number of electrons in outer energy level: ___7___
Ion formed by (gain/loss) ___gain___ of ___1___ electron(s)
Symbol for ion: ___F⁻___

9; 7; gain, one; F⁻

98. Complete the table for the sulfur atom:

Symbol for sulfur: $\underline{S}$
Atomic number: $\underline{16}$
Mass number: $\underline{32}$
Symbol of ion: $\underline{S^{2-}}$

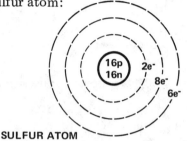

SULFUR ATOM

S; 16; 32; S^{2-}

99. What ions are formed from the following atoms?

Oxygen (atomic number 8): $\underline{O^{2-}}$

Chlorine (atomic number 17): $\underline{Cl^{-}}$

Hydrogen (atomic number 1): $\underline{H^{+}}$

Sodium (atomic number 11): $\underline{Na^{+}}$

O^{2-}; Cl^-; H^+; Na^+

100. Atoms with four or five electrons in their outer energy levels usually do not form ions. These we shall discuss later.

Atoms with eight electrons in their valence shells are stable. They do not have to gain or lose electrons. So you would expect these stable atoms to be:

_____ very reactive
__✓__ inert (unreactive)

---

inert (unreactive)

101. The sodium atom, atomic number 11, has how many electron(s) in its outer energy level? ___1___

The sodium atom will tend to lose the one electron in its outer energy level to form an ion with a charge of___+1___.

1; +1

102. The chlorine atom, which has the symbol __Cl___, has atomic number 17. It has how many electrons in its outer energy level? ___7___

The chlorine atom will tend to gain (how many?) ___1___ electron(s) to form an ion with a charge of __-1___.

Cl; 7; 1; -1

103. Fill in the diagram to show the reaction between sodium and chlorine.

__Na__ + __Cl__ ⟶ __Na+__ + __Cl−__

39

$$Na + Cl \longrightarrow Na^+ + Cl^-$$

104. The sodium ion and the chloride ion are oppositely charged. These ions are held together by the attraction of their opposite charges. We say that there is an *ionic bond* between the sodium ion and the chloride ion.

An ionic bond is produced whenever one atom loses an electron or electrons and another atom __gains__ the electron or electrons.

---

gains

105. In the reaction

$$Zn + S \longrightarrow Zn^{2+} + S^{2-}$$

the zinc ion and the sulfur ion are held together by an __ionic bond__.

---

ionic bond

106. When a sodium atom combines with a chlorine atom, according to the following equation:

$$Na + Cl \longrightarrow Na^+ + Cl^-$$

a compound containing a positively charged sodium __ion__ and a __negatively__ charged chloride __ion__ is formed.

This compound (sodium chloride) is usually written as NaCl, with the charges being understood and not written.

---

ion, negatively, ion

107. When the compound NaCl is placed in water, the ionic bond holding the sodium ion and the chloride ion together is weakened, so that these ions are free to move throughout the solution.

Therefore, NaCl in water produces a *solution* containing sodium ions (Na^+) and __choride__ ions (__Cl^-__).

---

chloride; Cl^-

108. When the compound HCl is placed in water, it produces a solution containing __Hydrogen__ ions (__H^+__) and __chloride__ ions (__Cl^-__).

When the compound H_2SO_4 is placed in water, it produces a solution containing __Hydrogen (H^+)__ ions and SO_4^{2-} ions.

---

hydrogen, H^+, chloride, Cl^-; hydrogen (H^+)

109. Any substance that yields hydrogen ions (H^+) in solution is called an *acid*.

$$HCl \longrightarrow H^+ + Cl^-$$
$$H_2SO_4 \longrightarrow 2H^+ + SO_4^{2-}$$
$$HNO_3 \longrightarrow H^+ + NO_3^-$$

HNO_3 is an *acid* because it yields __hydrogen ions__ in solution.

hydrogen ions or H⁺

110. When the compound NaOH (sodium hydroxide) is placed in
water, sodium ions (Na⁺) and hydroxide ions (OH⁻) are present.

When the compound KOH (potassium hydroxide) is placed in
water, potassium ions (___K⁺___) and _hydroxide_ ions
(___OH⁻___) are present.

Complete the reaction:

KOH ⟶ ___K⁺___ + ___OH⁻___

K⁺, hydroxide, OH⁻;   KOH⟶K⁺ + OH⁻

111. The compounds KOH and NaOH: (check one)

_____ are acids because they yield hydrogen ions in
solution
___✓___ are not acids because they do not yield hydrogen
ions in solution

---

are not acids because they do not yield hydrogen ions in solution

112. Compounds that yield *hydroxide ions* (OH⁻) in solution are
called *bases*.

$$HNO_3 \longrightarrow H^+ + NO_3^-$$

This compound is (a base/an acid) ___an acid___ because
it yields ___Hydrogen___ ions in solution

42

an acid, hydrogen

113. $Ca(OH)_2 \longrightarrow Ca^{2+} + 2OH^-$

This compound is (a base/an acid) ___base___ because it
yields _hydroxid_ ions in solution.

---

a base, hydroxide

114. When the compound NaCl is placed in water, it yields
sodium ions and _chloride_ ions.

---

sodium (or Na^+), chloride (or Cl^-)

115. The solution of NaCl in water would not be considered an
acid because:

　　　　　　　　　　_____ a. it yields OH^- ions
　　　　　　　　　　_____ b. it doesn't break up into ions
　　　　　　　　　　___✓___ c. it yields no hydrogen ions

---

c. it yields no hydrogen ions

116. Compounds that yield hydrogen ions in solution are called
___acids___.

Compounds that yield hydroxide ions in solution are called
___bases___.

acids; bases

117. A compound that yields ions other than hydrogen ions or
hydroxide ions in solution is called a *salt*.

The following compounds yield ions in solution as indicated.
Are they acids, bases, or salts?

a. $Na_2CO_3 \longrightarrow 2Na^+ + CO_3^{2-}$ a.   _salt_

b. $Ca(OH)_2 \longrightarrow Ca^{2+} + 2OH^-$ b.   _base_

c. $MgCl_2 \longrightarrow Mg^{2+} + 2Cl^-$ c.   _salt_

d. $H_2SO_4 \longrightarrow 2H^+ + SO_4^{2-}$ d.   _acid_

e. $KOH \longrightarrow K^+ + OH^-$ e.   _base_

f. $NH_4OH \longrightarrow NH_4^+ + OH^-$ f.   _base_

a. salt; b. base; c. salt; d. acid; e. base; f. base

Electrolytes and Non-Electrolytes

118. We have discussed three kinds of compounds that produce
ions in solution:

a. H^+ ions are produced by compounds called _acids_.
b. OH^- ions are produced by compounds called _bases_.
c. Compounds that produce ions other than H^+ and OH^- are called _salts_.

---

a. acids; b. bases; c. salts

119. A solution that contains ions is called an *electrolyte* because it conducts electricity.

Would a solution of HCl, an acid, be an electrolyte? _yes_

$$HCl \longrightarrow H^+ + Cl^-$$

---

yes

120. Not all compounds produce ions in solution. Because solutions without ions *do not* conduct electricity, they are called *non-electrolytes.*

Here's what happens when magnesium chloride is put in solution:

$$MgCl_2 \longrightarrow Mg^{2+} + 2Cl^-$$

Does the solution of $MgCl_2$ contain ions? _yes_
The solution is: (check one)

_____✓____ an electrolyte
_____ a non-electrolyte

Would this solution conduct electricity? _yes_

45

Is MgCl$_2$ an acid, a base, or a salt? __salt__
(If necessary, check frames 116 and 117.)

---

yes; an electrolyte; yes; a salt

121. Since acids, bases, and salts yield ions in solution, they are
called __electrolytes__.

Alcohol does not yield ions in solution, so it is called __non-
electrolyte__.

---

electrolytes; a non-electrolyte

pH

122. The acid or basic strength of a solution may be expressed in
terms of a number called the *pH* of that solution. The pH scale
expresses the concentration of hydrogen ions (and hydroxide ions)
in solution.

The pH range is from 0 to 14, with a pH of 7 indicating a neutral
solution. A pH below 7 indicates an *acid* solution.

a.   A pH of 3 indicates a(n) __acid__ solution.
b.   A pH of 7 indicates a(n) __neutral__ solution.
c.   A pH of 6 indicates a(n) __acid__ solution.

a. acid;   b. neutral;   c. acid

123. Although all pH's below 7 indicate acid solutions, there is a definite progression of acid strengths according to pH values.

A pH between 5 and 7 indicates a weak acid solution, between 2 and 5 indicates a moderately strong acid solution, between 0 and 2 indicates a strong acid solution, as shown in the following chart:

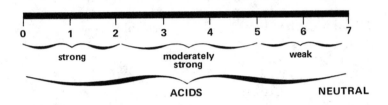

124. a.   Which of the following pH's indicates a solution containing a strong acid?
4, 7, 1, 6 ____1____

b.   Which of the following pH's indicates a solution containing a moderately strong acid?
4, 7, 1, 6 ____4____

c.   A pH of 0 indicates what strength acid solution? ___Strong___

d.   A pH of 3 indicates what strength acid solution? ___moderate___

a. 1;   b. 4;   c. strong;   d. moderately strong

125. pH values may be indicated as decimal values, as well as whole numbers. Thus, a pH of 2.56 indicates a solution whose pH lies between 2 and 3, and is, thus, a:

    _____ a. strong acid solution
    _____ b. weak acid solution
    ___✓___ c. moderately strong acid solution

---

c.   moderately strong acid solution

126. Among the following pH's, which solution contains a weak acid?

    _____ 1.72   _____ 2.00
    _____ 3.75   ___✓___ 6.27

6.27

127. Among the following pH's, which solution contains a strong acid?

    ___✓___ 1.72   _____ 5.00
    _____ 3.75   _____ 6.38
    _____ 7.00

1.72

128. Of solutions with these pH's, which one is neutral?

    _____ 2.70   _____ 5.00
    _____ 4.65   ___✓___ 7.00

7.00

129. A solution whose pH is above 7 is called a *basic* solution.

A solution whose pH is between 7 and 9 is called a weak basic solution, between 9 and 12 is called a moderately strong basic solution, between 12 and 14 is called a strong basic solution, as shown in the following chart:

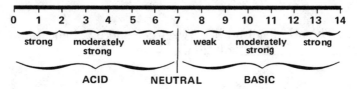

Of the following pH's, which indicates a strong basic solution?

_____ 3.5   ✓ 13.9
_____ 7.0   _____ 6.4
_____ 9.5

13.9

130. Of the following pH's, which indicates a weak basic solution?

_____ 2.7   _____ 10.8
✓ 8.3   _____ 14.0
_____ 4.2

8.3

131. Which of the following pH's indicates a moderately strong basic solution?

_____ 2.2   ✓_____ 11.1
_____ 4.7   _____ 13.7

11.1

132. The pH of saliva lies between 5.5 and 6.9, indicating a
weak acid solution.

---

weak acid

133. Bile has a pH range of 7.8 to 8.6, so it is a _weak_
basic solution.

---

weak basic

134. Urine has a pH range of 5.5 to 6.9, so it is a _weak_
acid solution.

---

weak acid

135. The gastric juices have a pH range of 1.6 to 1.8, so they
make up a _strong acid_ solution.

50

strong acid

136. Blood has a pH range of 7.35 to 7.45, so it is a __weak__ __basic__ solution.

---

weak basic

137. The pancreatic juices have a pH range of 7.5 to 8.0, so they make up a __weak basic__ solution.

---

weak basic

Catalysts and Enzymes

138. Look at these two chemical reactions.

$$2\ KClO_3 \xrightarrow{\text{heat}} 2\ KCl\ +\ 3\ O_2 \text{ (slow reaction)}$$

$$2\ KClO_3\ +\ MnO_2 \xrightarrow{\text{heat}} 2\ KCl\ +\ 3\ O_2\ +\ MnO_2 \text{ (fast reaction)}$$

In the second reaction, is the MnO_2 changed or used up? __no__

Does the MnO_2 affect the speed of the reaction (since all the other factors are the same)? __yes__

MnO_2 is called a *catalyst*.

no; yes

139. A *catalyst* is a substance that changes the speed of a chemical reaction without being used up itself. Catalysts are usually non-specific—they can change the speed of many different reactions.

Catalysts are important in reactions involving both substances that are not living or not derived from living organisms, and those that are living or are so derived. The *specific* catalysts for *living organisms* are called *enzymes.*

Pepsin is an enzyme found in the gastric juices. It speeds up the reaction for the digestion of protein in the stomach. Note that pepsin is an enzyme for a particular substance—protein. In general, enzymes are highly specific; catalysts are nonspecific.

A substance that speeds up a chemical reaction in a nonliving substance is called _catalyst_.

A substance that speeds up a chemical reaction in a living substance is called _enzyme_.

___

a catalyst; an enzyme

140. An enzyme is a molecule of irregular shape. Although it doesn't look like this in reality, one small part of it might be represented like this:

ENZYME

If two compounds, A and B, approach the enzyme, they can attach themselves to it, then react together and go off as a compound, AB. The enzyme is left free to react again and is not used up.

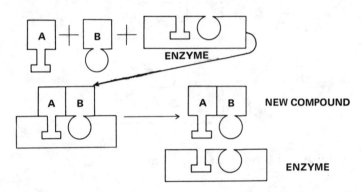

Enzymes are (specific/nonspecific) _specific_ catalysts that _increase_ the rate of chemical reaction in living systems.

---

specific, increase

141. Notice the shape of the hypothetical enzyme indicated below:

Two substances, A and B , can attach themselves to the

enzyme to form compound

53

The specificity of the enzyme is believed to be due to its particular shape. Suppose that the enzyme had the shape

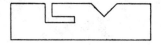

or the shape

could A and B react on it to form AB? _No_

We say in this case that an active site of the enzyme has been distorted. If this were true, would the activity of the enzyme be increased, decreased, or destroyed? _destroyed_

---

no; destroyed

54

III
THE COVALENT BOND

142. You've already learned that atoms tend to lose electrons to form positively charged ions if they have 1, ____2____ or ____3____ electrons in their outer energy levels.

On the other hand, atoms that have ____6____ or ____7____ electrons in their outer energy levels tend to gain electrons to form ____negative____ charged ions.

2, 3; 6, 7, negatively

143. Answer these questions about the atoms shown at the top of the next page.

a. Which of the atoms will lose electron(s) to form positively charged ions? ____Mg, Al, H____

b. Which of the atoms will gain electron(s) to form negatively charged ions? ____S, Cl____

c. Which of the atoms has a complete outer energy level? ____Ne____

d. You know that such elements with a complete outer energy level are usually: (check one) ____ *unstable and reactive,* or
____✓____*stable and unreactive.*

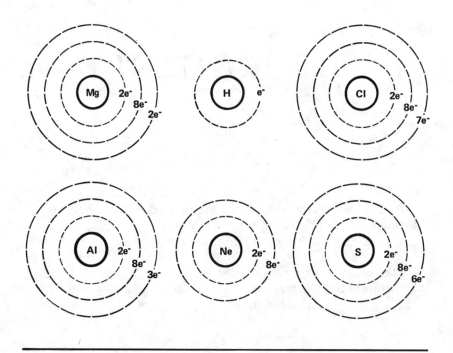

a. H, Mg, Al;   b. Cl, S;   c. Ne;   d. stable and unreactive

144. Atoms with four or five electrons in their outer energy levels tend to *share* electrons.

When atoms share electrons, they form a *covalent bond.*

Which of the atoms below would form covalent bonds? C, N

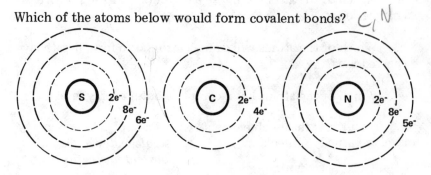

C and N

145. When two atoms share electrons, they are held together by a
Covalent bond.

When two atoms share electrons, no ions are produced. Will the
resulting compound be an electrolyte or a non-electrolyte?
non-electrolyte

---

covalent; non-electrolyte

146. Atoms with four or five electrons in their outer energy levels
tend to share electrons, but under some conditions those with more
or fewer electrons in their outer energy levels may also share electrons.

When one atom loses an electron and another atom gains that
electron, the ions thus formed are held together by:

_✓_ an ionic bond
_____ a covalent bond

---

an ionic bond

147. Compounds containing ionic bonds will be (electrolytes/
non-electrolytes) _electrolyte_.

Compounds containing only covalent bonds will be (electrolytes/
non-electrolytes) _non-electrolytes_

57

electrolytes; non-electrolytes

148. The carbon atom, atomic number 6, has 4 electrons in its outer energy level.

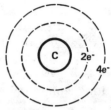

Since the carbon atom has 4 electrons in its outer energy level, it needs __4__ more electrons to become stable. It can get these electrons by *sharing*. The 4 electrons in the outer energy level of the carbon atom may be represented as below, with one dot for each electron in the valence shell.

$$\bullet \ \text{C} \ \bullet$$

4

149. When atoms share electrons, they always try to reach stable configurations of 8 electrons in the outer energy levels.

The only exception to this rule is the hydrogen atom, which reaches a stable configuration when it has two electrons in its outer energy level, which is also its only energy level. This first energy level can hold only __2__ electrons.

2

150. Consider the carbon atom with 4 electrons in its outer energy level. With how many hydrogen atoms can it share electrons to reach a stable configuration of 8 electrons in its outer energy level?

__4__

151. The four hydrogen atoms can share electrons with a carbon atom to form a compound of the following type:

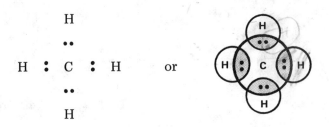

There are ___8___ electrons around the carbon atom and ___2___ electrons around each hydrogen atom.

8, 2

152. When two hydrogen atoms combine, they share electrons to form

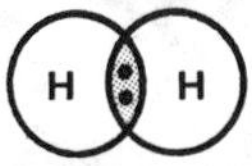

Each hydrogen atom then has ___2___ electrons around it.

2

153. In this compound, what is the total number of covalent bonds?

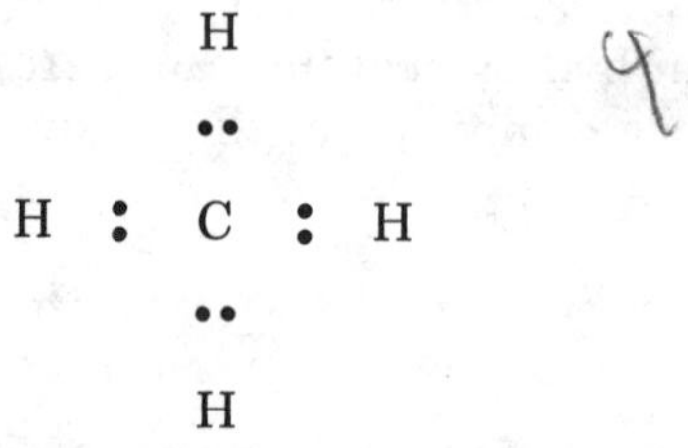

H

••

H **:** C **:** H

••

H

4

154. The chlorine atom, atomic number 17, has _____ electrons in its outer energy level.

The electrons in the outer energy level of the chlorine atom may be indicated as

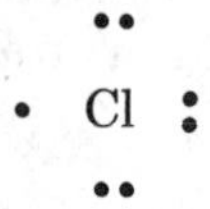

••

• Cl **:**

••

When 2 chlorine atoms combine, they share electrons to reach a stable configuration of 8 electrons in the outer energy level of each atom, or

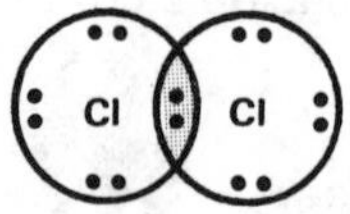

7

155. What type of bond is there between the two chlorine atoms? _____.

covalent

156. The covalent bond is frequently indicated by a short line rather than by dots; thus, the hydrogen molecule may be represented as

$$H : H \text{ or } H - H$$

The short line indicates a pair of shared electrons.

The compound CH_4 may be represented either as

<pre>
        H   H
        •• |
  H : C : H   or   H — C — H
        •• |
        H   H
</pre>

Complete the second representation of the chlorine molecule, Cl_2.

<pre>
    ••   ••
: Cl : Cl : or   Cl — Cl
    ••   ••
</pre>

Cl—Cl

157. The carbon atom, atomic number 6, needs how many electrons to complete its outer energy level? ___4___

Since the carbon atom has 4 electrons in its outer energy level, and since it will tend to share these electrons, how many covalent bonds will a carbon atom form? ___4___.

4; 4

158. The carbon atom, therefore, must have four covalent bonds, or must have four bonds attached to it. These bonds may be indicated as follows:

$$-\overset{|}{\underset{|}{C}}- \qquad -\overset{|}{C}= \qquad -C\equiv \qquad C\equiv$$

Note that each carbon atom has four bonds attached to it, regardless of how the bonds are arranged.

The hydrogen atom has one electron in its outer energy level, the first energy level. When the hydrogen atom shares electrons, how many more does it need to complete that outer energy level?

1

1

159. The oxygen atom, atomic number 8, has ___6___ electrons in its outer energy level.

When the oxygen atom shares electrons, how many more electrons does it need to complete its outer energy level? ___2___

Therefore, each oxygen atom must have how many bonds attached to it? ___2___

6; 2; 2

160. Draw the structure of the compound formed when four hydrogen atoms form bonds with a central carbon atom.

$$H-\overset{\overset{\displaystyle H}{|}}{\underset{\underset{\displaystyle H}{|}}{C}}-H$$

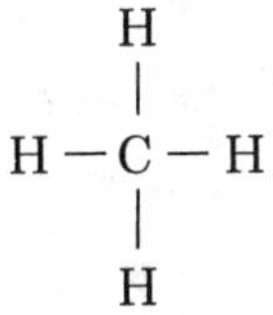

```
      H
      |
H — C — H
      |
      H
```

161. Consider the following arrangement of carbon atoms:

$$C - C$$

This arrangement indicates a bond or a shared electron pair between two carbon atoms.

How many hydrogen atoms may be attached to the left carbon atom? _3_

How many hydrogen atoms may be attached to the right carbon atom? _3_

3; 3

162. Diagram all the hydrogen atoms attached to this structure:

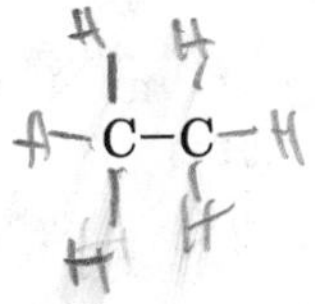

```
   H   H
   |   |
H— C — C — H
   |   |
   H   H
```

Check the total number of bonds. How many bonds does each carbon atom have? __4__

How many bonds does each hydrogen atom have? __1__

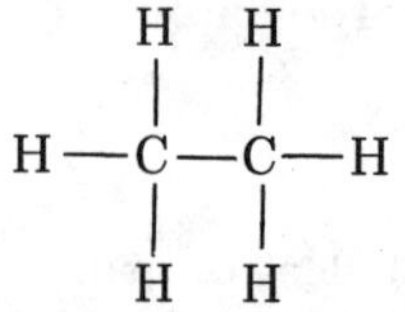

4; 1

163. Consider this arrangement of carbon atoms:

$$C - C - C$$

a.   How many hydrogen atoms may be attached to the left carbon atom? __3__
b.   How many hydrogen atoms may be attached to the center carbon atom? __2__
c.   How many hydrogen atoms may be attached to the right carbon atom? __3__

---

a.   3; b. 2;   c. 3

164. Diagram the compound containing three attached carbon atoms, indicating all the hydrogen atoms connected to those carbon atoms.

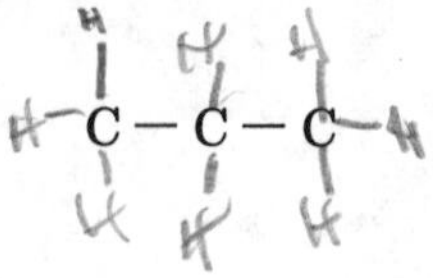

```
    H   H   H
    |   |   |
H — C — C — C — H
    |   |   |
    H   H   H
```

165. Consider this arrangement of carbon atoms:

```
          C
          |
    C  —  C  —  C
          |
          C
```

a.   How many hydrogen atoms may be attached to the right carbon atom? _____

b.   How many hydrogen atoms may be attached to the left carbon atom? _____

c.   How many hydrogen atoms may be attached to the upper carbon atom? _____

d.   How many hydrogen atoms may be attached to the lower carbon atom? _____

e.   How many hydrogen atoms may be attached to the center carbon atom? _____

---

a. 3; b. 3; c. 3; d. 3; e. 0 (or none)

166. Diagram the structure of the compound containing the following arrangement of carbon atoms, indicating all the hydrogen atoms.

Why can there be no hydrogen atoms on the center carbon atom?

It has 4 bonds to carbons

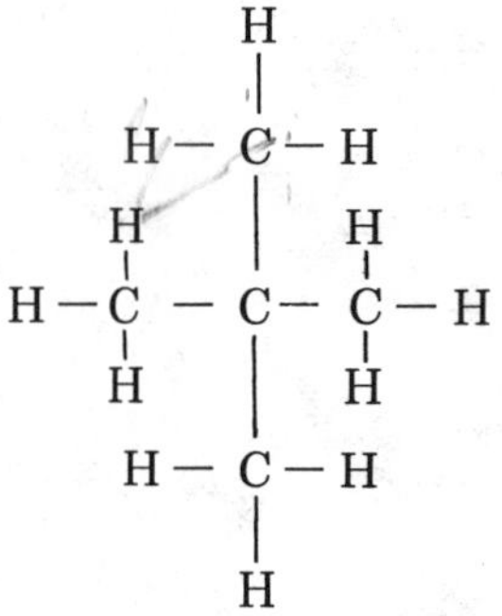

H
|
H — C — H
H | H
| | |
H — C — C — C — H
| | |
H | H
H — C — H
|
H

It already has four bonds.

167. Consider the following arrangement of carbon atoms:

$$C = C$$

There are two bonds (a double bond) between the carbon atoms.

A bond (a single bond) represents one shared pair of electrons.

A double bond represents _2 pairs of shared electrons_

---

two shared pairs of electrons

168. To become stable, the carbon atom must form how many covalent bonds? _4_

In the structure below, how many hydrogen atoms may be attached to the left carbon atom? _2_

$$C = C$$

In the space below, diagram the structure of the compound containing two **carbon** atoms connected by a double bond. Show all of the hydrogen atoms.

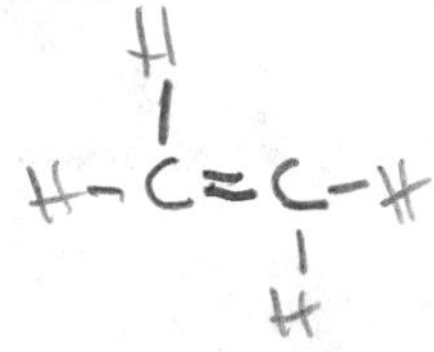

$$H-C=C-H$$
(with H above and below, handwritten: $H-C \equiv C-H$ with H on top and bottom)

When you have completed your diagram, check it by counting the number of bonds around each carbon atom.

4; 2

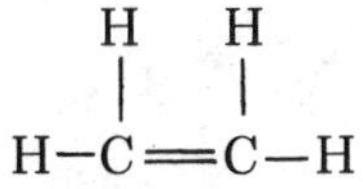

$$
\begin{array}{cc}
\text{H} & \text{H} \\
| & | \\
\text{H}-\text{C} &\!\!=\!\!\text{C}-\text{H}
\end{array}
$$

169. Consider the following arrangement of carbon atoms:

$$C = C-C$$

a.   How many hydrogen atoms may be attached to the left carbon atom? __2__
b.   How many hydrogen atoms may be attached to the center carbon atom? __1__
c.   How many hydrogen atoms may be attached to the right carbon atom? __3__

---

a. 2;   b. 1;   c. 3

170. Complete the structure of the compound at the right, showing all the hydrogen atoms.

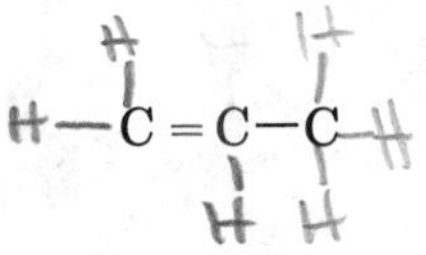

$$H-C=C-C-H$$
(handwritten completion with H atoms)

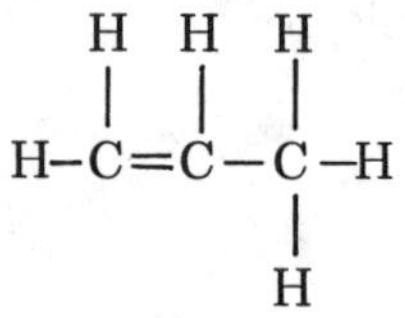

```
      H  H  H
      |  |  |
  H–C=C – C –H
            |
            H
```

171. Consider the following arrangement of carbon atoms:

$$C–C=C–C$$

a.   How many hydrogen atoms may be attached to the left carbon atom? ___3___
b.   How many hydrogen atoms may be attached to the carbon atom at left center? ___1___
c.   How many hydrogen atoms may be attached to the carbon atom at right center? ___1___
d.   How many hydrogen atoms may be attached to the far right carbon atom? ___3___

---

a. 3;   b. 1;   c. 1;   d. 3

172. Complete the structure of the following compound, showing all the hydrogen atoms.

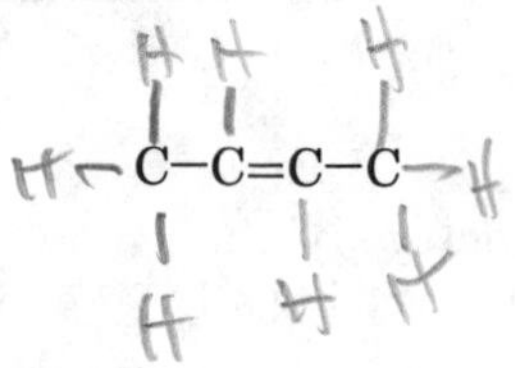

```
        H  H      H
        |  |      |
  H – C–C=C–C – H
        |  |  |
        H  H  H
```

Check your diagram. How many bonds should each carbon atom have? __4__

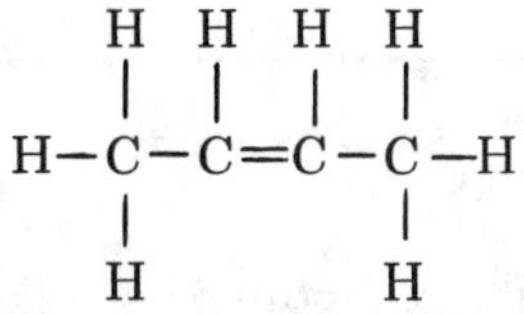

```
      H   H   H   H              4
      |   |   |   |
  H—C—C=C—C—H
      |       |
      H       H
```

173. Consider the following arrangement of carbon atoms:

$$C \equiv C$$

There are three bonds (a triple bond) between the two carbon atoms.

A single bond represents one pair of shared electrons.

A double bond represents __2 pairs of shared electrons__.

A triple bond represents __3 pairs of shared electrons__.

---

two pairs of shared electrons; three pairs of shared electrons

174. In the structure below, how many hydrogen atoms may be attached to each carbon atom? __1__

$$C \equiv C$$

1

175. Complete the structure below, adding all the necessary hydrogen atoms.

$$\overset{\displaystyle H}{\underset{\displaystyle}{\overset{\displaystyle |}{C}}} \equiv C \diagdown \underset{\displaystyle H}{}$$

H−C≡C−H

176. Complete the structure of the following compound:

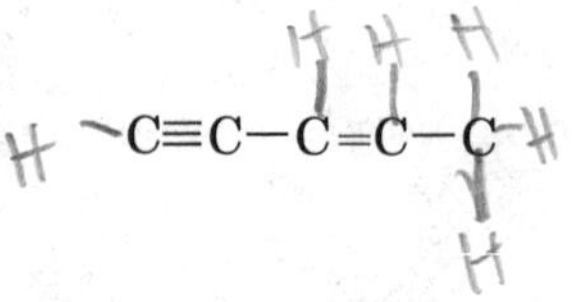

$$H \diagup C \equiv C - \overset{H}{\underset{}{C}} = \overset{H}{\underset{}{C}} - \overset{H}{\underset{H}{C}} H$$

Check your diagram for the correct number of bonds around each carbon atom.

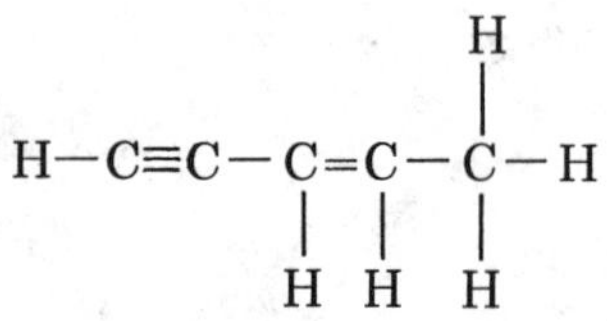

$$\begin{array}{ccccccc} & & & & & H & \\ & & & & & | & \\ H-C \equiv C- & C & = & C & - & C & -H \\ & & | & & | & & | \\ & & H & & H & & H \end{array}$$

177. Complete the structure of the following compounds by adding the necessary hydrogen atoms:

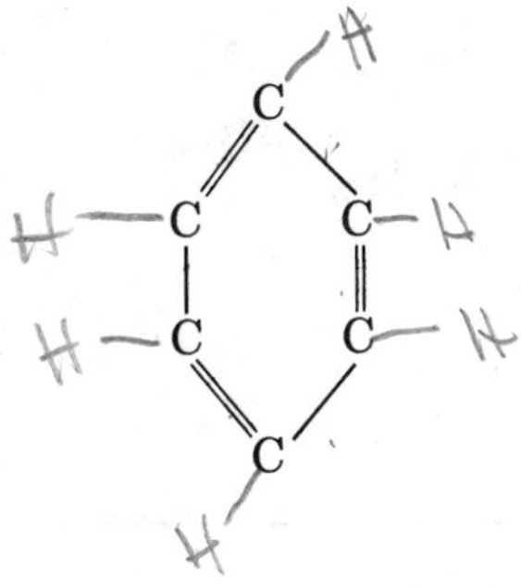

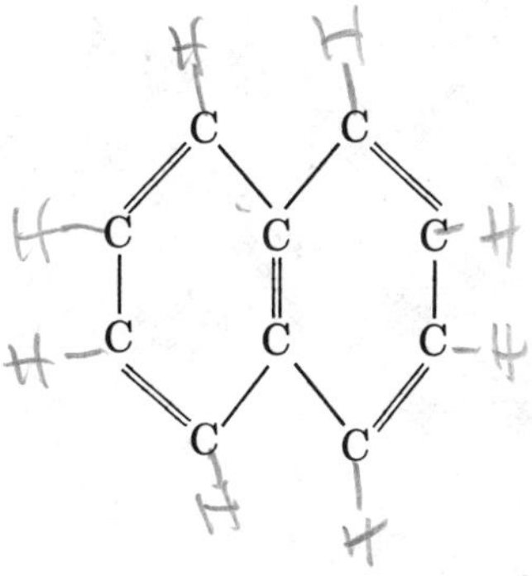

Check the number of bonds around each carbon atom.

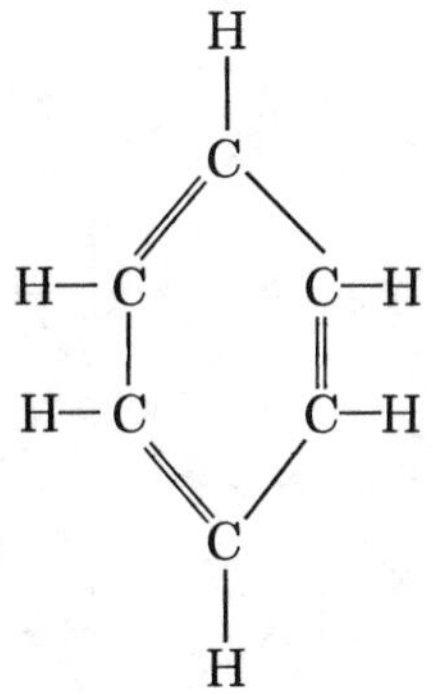

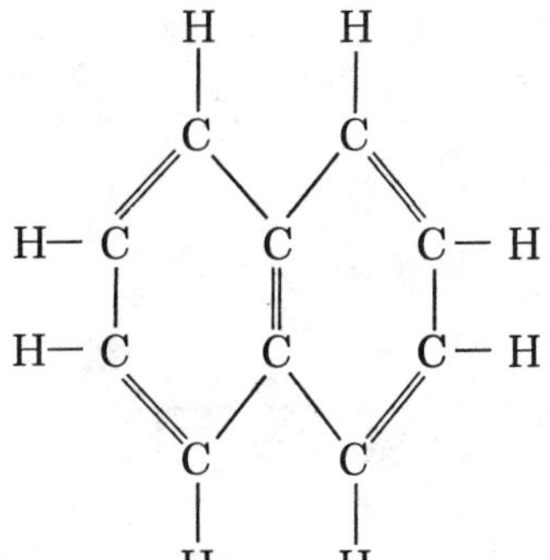

178. Diagram the structure of carbon tetrachloride, CCl_4, in which each chlorine atom has one bond attached to it.

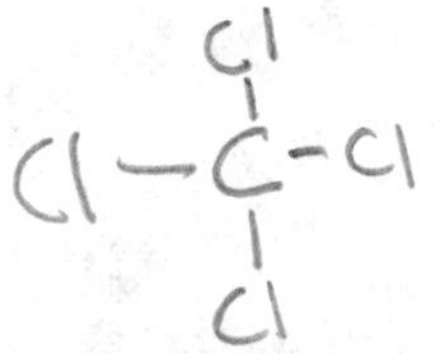

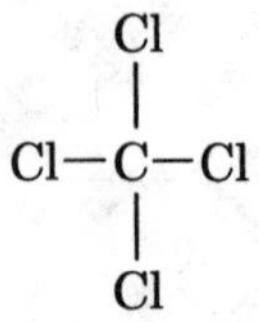

$$Cl-\overset{\displaystyle Cl}{\underset{\displaystyle Cl}{C}}-Cl$$

$$Cl-\overset{\displaystyle Cl}{\underset{\displaystyle Cl}{C}}-Cl$$

179. Diagram the structure of chloroform, $CHCl_3$.

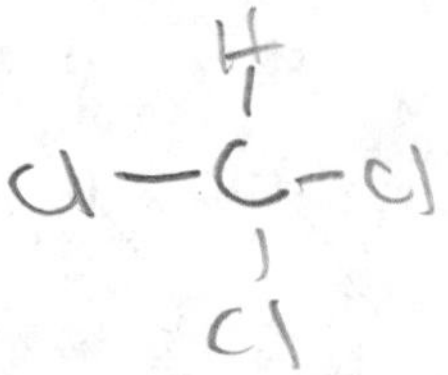

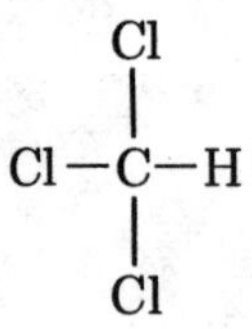

$$Cl-\overset{\displaystyle H}{\underset{\displaystyle Cl}{C}}-Cl$$

$$Cl-\overset{\displaystyle Cl}{\underset{\displaystyle Cl}{C}}-H$$

72

180. Nitrogen, atomic number 7, has ___5___ electrons in its outer energy level and so must have ___3___ bonds attached to it.

Diagram the ammonia molecule, NH_3.

$$
\begin{array}{c}
H \\
| \\
N-H \\
| \\
H
\end{array}
$$

5; 3

$$
\begin{array}{c}
H \\
| \\
N-H \\
| \\
H
\end{array}
$$

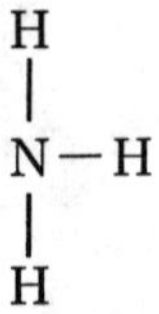

181. Note the following structure:

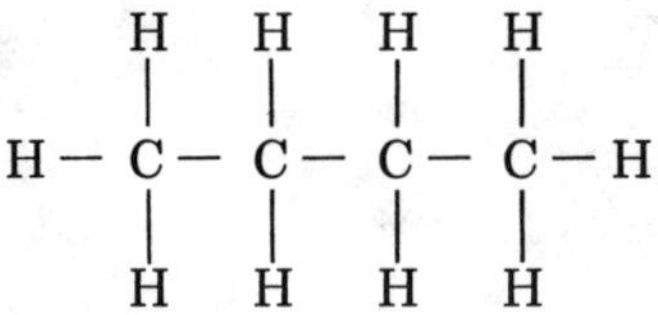

$$
\begin{array}{ccccccc}
 & H & H & H & H \\
 & | & | & | & | \\
H- & C- & C- & C- & C-H \\
 & | & | & | & | \\
 & H & H & H & H
\end{array}
$$

It may be simplified and written as

$$CH_3CH_2CH_2CH_3$$

73

Likewise,

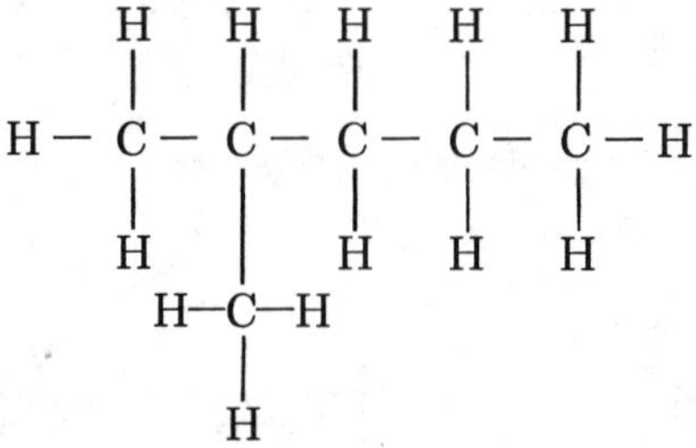

$$\begin{array}{ccccccccc}
& \text{H} & & \text{H} & & \text{H} & & \text{H} & & \text{H} \\
& | & & | & & | & & | & & | \\
\text{H}- & \text{C} & - & \text{C} & - & \text{C} & - & \text{C} & - & \text{C} & -\text{H} \\
& | & & | & & | & & | & & | \\
& \text{H} & & | & & \text{H} & & \text{H} & & \text{H} \\
& & & \text{H}-\text{C}-\text{H} \\
& & & | \\
& & & \text{H}
\end{array}$$

may be simplified and written as

$$CH_3CH(CH_3)CH_2CH_2CH_3$$

and

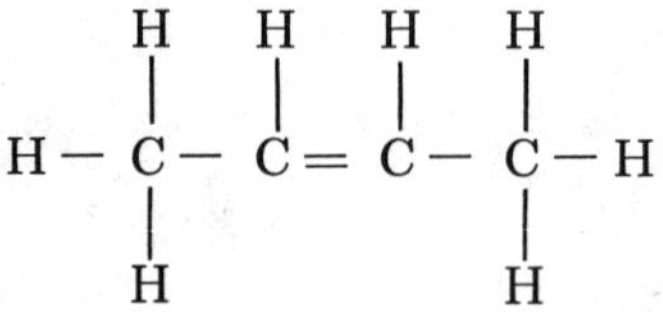

$$\begin{array}{ccccccc}
& \text{H} & & \text{H} & & \text{H} & & \text{H} \\
& | & & | & & | & & | \\
\text{H}- & \text{C} & - & \text{C} & = & \text{C} & - & \text{C} & -\text{H} \\
& | & & & & & & | \\
& \text{H} & & & & & & \text{H}
\end{array}$$

may be simplified and written as

$$CH_3CH{=}CHCH_3$$

182. How may the following structures be written in simplified form?

a. 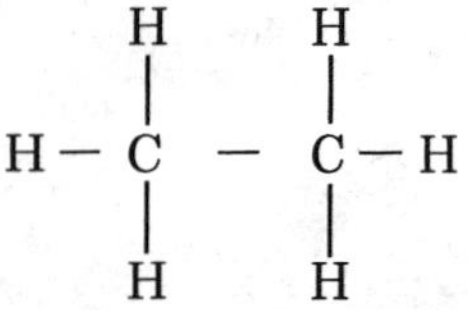
$$\begin{array}{ccccc}
& \text{H} & & \text{H} \\
& | & & | \\
\text{H}- & \text{C} & - & \text{C} & -\text{H} \\
& | & & | \\
& \text{H} & & \text{H}
\end{array}$$
$$\underline{CH_3\,CH_3}$$

b. 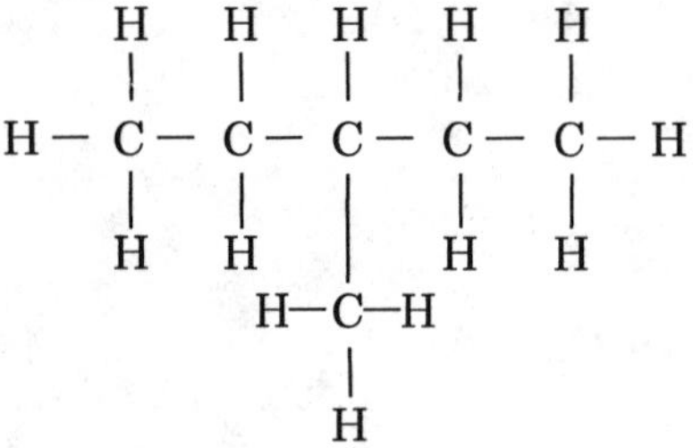
$$\begin{array}{ccccccccc}
& \text{H} & & \text{H} & & \text{H} & & \text{H} & & \text{H} \\
& | & & | & & | & & | & & | \\
\text{H}- & \text{C} & - & \text{C} & - & \text{C} & - & \text{C} & - & \text{C} & -\text{H} \\
& | & & | & & | & & | & & | \\
& \text{H} & & \text{H} & & | & & \text{H} & & \text{H} \\
& & & & & \text{H}-\text{C}-\text{H} \\
& & & & & | \\
& & & & & \text{H}
\end{array}$$
$$\underline{CH_3CH_2CH(CH_3)CH_2CH_3}$$

74

c.
$$H-\underset{\underset{H}{|}}{\overset{\overset{H}{|}}{C}}-C\equiv C-H$$

$\underline{CH_3C\equiv CH}$

d.
$$H-\underset{\underset{H}{|}}{\overset{\overset{H}{|}}{C}}\underset{\underset{H-\overset{|}{C}-H}{|}}{\overset{\overset{H-\overset{|}{C}-H}{|}}{C}}\underset{\underset{H}{|}}{\overset{\overset{H}{|}}{C}}-\underset{\underset{H}{|}}{\overset{\overset{H}{|}}{C}}-H$$

$\underline{CH_3C(CH_3)_2\,CH_2CH_3}$

---

a. CH_3CH_3; b. $CH_3CH_2CH(CH_3)CH_2CH_3$; c. $CH_3C\equiv CH$;
d. $CH_3C(CH_3)_2CH_2CH_3$

183. The structure for benzene, C_6H_6,

$$
\begin{array}{c}
H \\
| \\
C \\
\diagup \hspace{0.3em} \diagdown \\
H-C \hspace{1.5em} C-H \\
\| \hspace{2em} \| \\
H-C \hspace{1.5em} C-H \\
\diagdown \hspace{0.3em} \diagup \\
C \\
| \\
H
\end{array}
$$

is usually abbreviated as

How would you abbreviate
the structure for:

a.

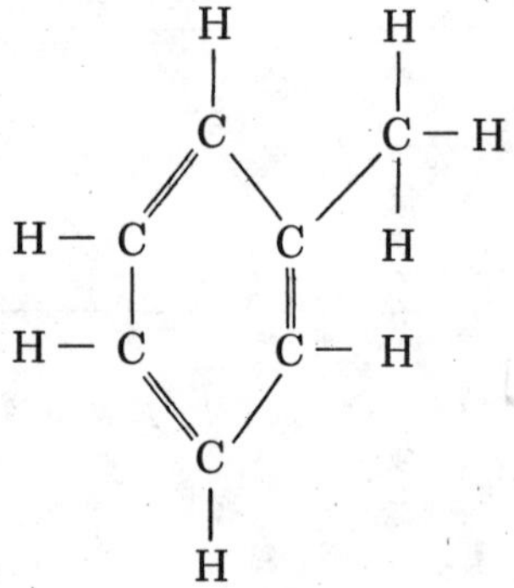

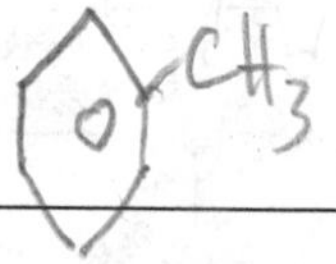

b.

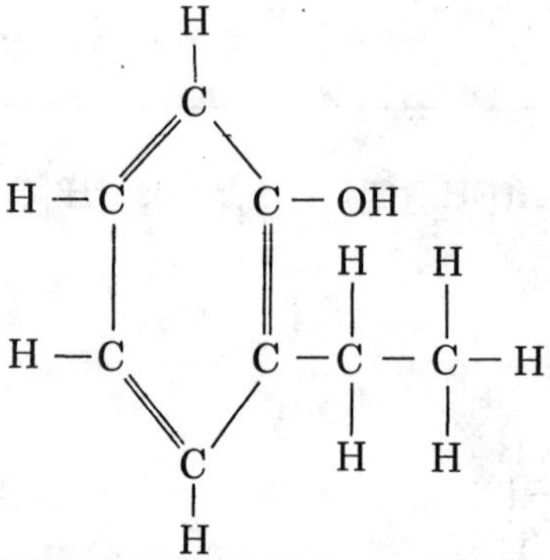

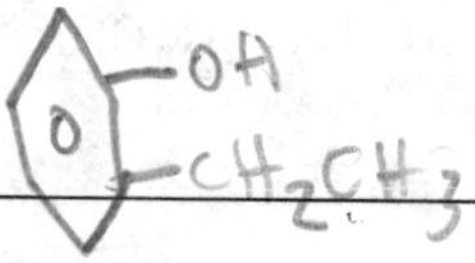

a. 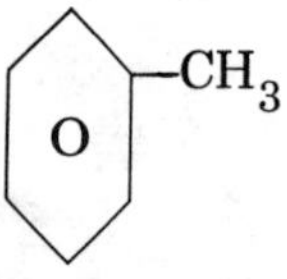 —CH₃

b. 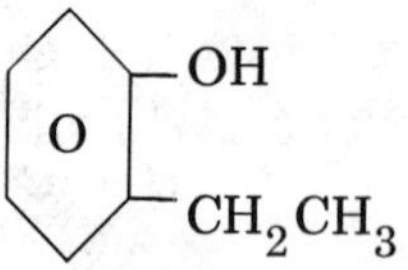 —OH

184. Draw the complete structure for each of the following
simplified formulas:

a. $CH_3CH_2CH_3$

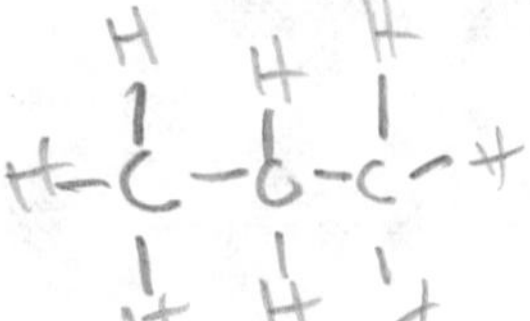

b.　$CH_3CH=CHCH_3$

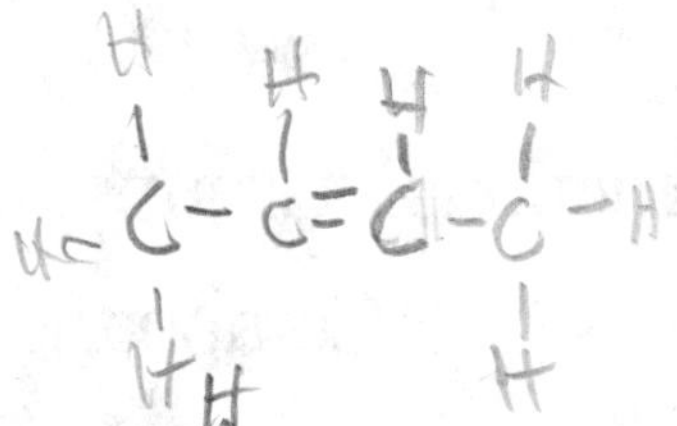

c.

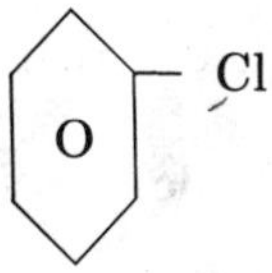

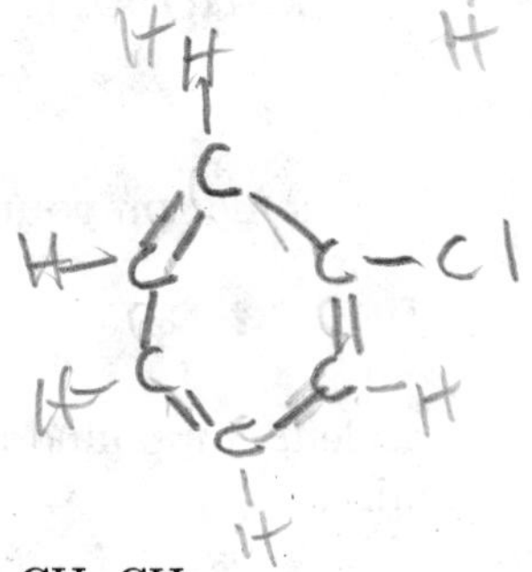

d.　$CH_3CH(CH_3)CH_2CH_2CH_3$

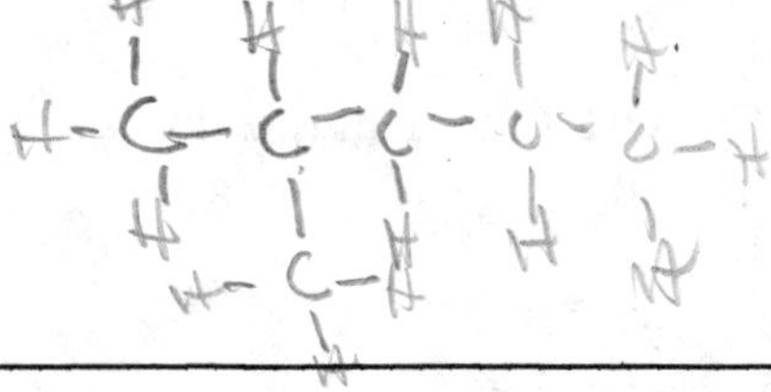

---

a.

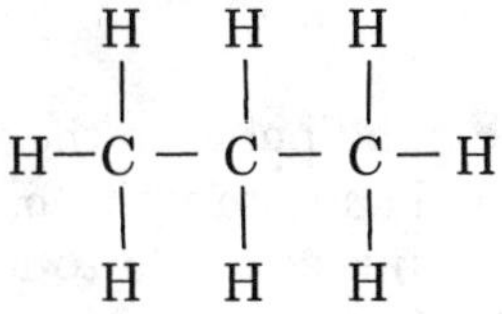

```
    H   H   H
    |   |   |
H — C — C — C — H
    |   |   |
    H   H   H
```

b.

```
    H   H   H   H
    |   |   |   |
H — C — C = C — C — H
    |           |
    H           H
```

c.

```
        H
        |
        C
       ⫽ \
H — C     C — Cl
    |     ‖
H — C     C — H
       \ ⫽
        C
        |
        H
```

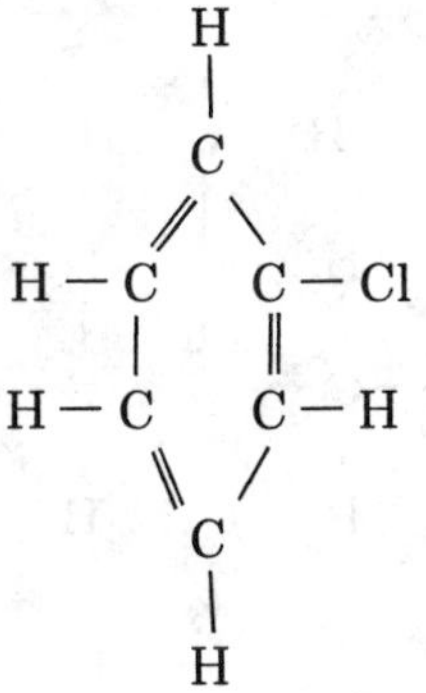

d.

```
    H   H   H   H   H
    |   |   |   |   |
H — C — C — C — C — C — H
    |   |   |   |   |
    H   |   H   H   H
        |
        H — C — H
            |
            H
```

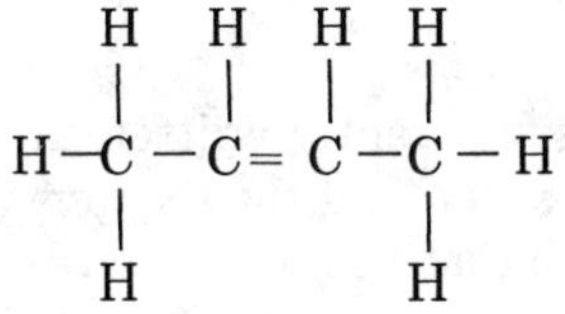

77

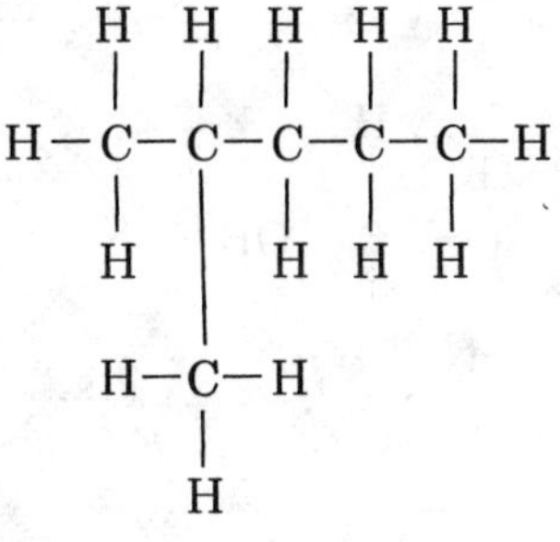

Functional Groups in Organic Compounds

185. The OH group in an ionic compound is called a hydroxide ion.

$$NaOH \longrightarrow Na^+ + OH^- \quad (Ionic)$$

The OH group in a covalent compound is called an *alcohol* group; it does not ionize.

$$H - \overset{\displaystyle H}{\underset{\displaystyle H}{\overset{|}{\underset{|}{C}}}} - OH \quad (Covalent,\ not\ ionized)$$

The OH group has the following bonds:

$$-O-H$$

It is frequently written as —OH, with the bond between the hydrogen and the oxygen being understood and not written. Note that the oxygen atom still has two bonds attached to it.

186. Check each compound that is an alcohol.

$$H - \overset{\displaystyle H}{\underset{\displaystyle H}{\overset{|}{\underset{|}{C}}}} - \overset{\displaystyle H}{\underset{\displaystyle H}{\overset{|}{\underset{|}{C}}}} - \overset{\displaystyle H}{\underset{\displaystyle H}{\overset{|}{\underset{|}{C}}}} - OH$$

_____ a.

$$H - \overset{\displaystyle H}{\underset{\displaystyle H}{\overset{|}{\underset{|}{C}}}} - H$$

$$H - \overset{\displaystyle H}{\underset{\displaystyle H}{\overset{|}{\underset{|}{C}}}} - \overset{|}{\underset{\displaystyle OH}{C}} - \overset{\displaystyle H}{\underset{\displaystyle H}{\overset{|}{\underset{|}{C}}}} - H$$

_____ b.

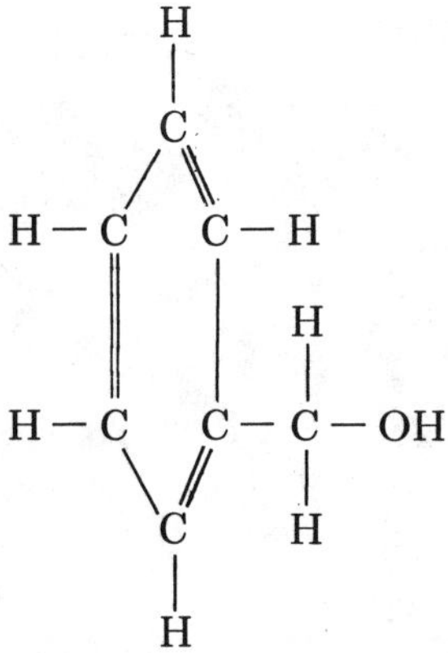

c.

$CH_3CH(OH)CH_3$

_____ d.

$CH_3CH_2CH_2CH(CH_3)CH_2OH$

_____ e.

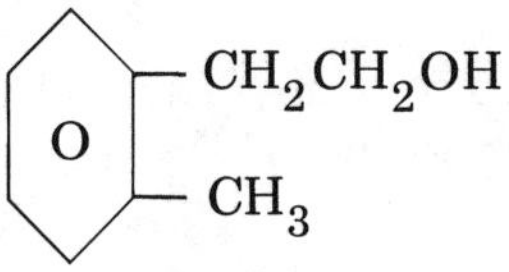

_____ f.

All of them (a, b, c, d, e, f)

187. A compound that contains a CHO group is called an *aldehyde*.

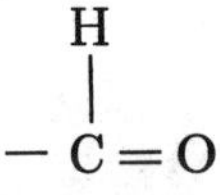

$$\overset{\displaystyle H}{\underset{}{-\,C=O}}$$

Note that in the aldehyde group the oxygen atom has a double bond attached to it.

188.

$$H - \overset{\displaystyle H}{\underset{\displaystyle H}{\overset{|}{\underset{|}{C}}}} - \overset{\displaystyle H}{\underset{\displaystyle H}{\overset{|}{\underset{|}{C}}}} - \overset{\displaystyle H}{\overset{|}{C}} = O$$

The compound above is an: (check one)

_____ alcohol
___✓___ aldehyde

---

aldehyde

189. Note that the above compound may also be written as

$$CH_3 CH_2 CHO$$

where the CHO group indicates an aldehyde. Note also that the aldehyde group is at the end of the molecule.

Check the correct name for each of the compounds in the next ten frames, and explain why you chose the answer you did.

190.

$$H - \overset{\displaystyle H}{\underset{\displaystyle H}{\overset{|}{\underset{|}{C}}}} - \overset{\displaystyle H}{\underset{\displaystyle H}{\overset{|}{\underset{|}{C}}}} - \overset{\displaystyle H}{\underset{\displaystyle H}{\overset{|}{\underset{|}{C}}}} - \overset{\displaystyle H}{\underset{\displaystyle H}{\overset{|}{\underset{|}{C}}}} - OH$$

___✓___ alcohol

_____ aldehyde

_____ some other type

Why? _Because it has a hydroxide on the end_

---

alcohol; It has an —OH group.

191.

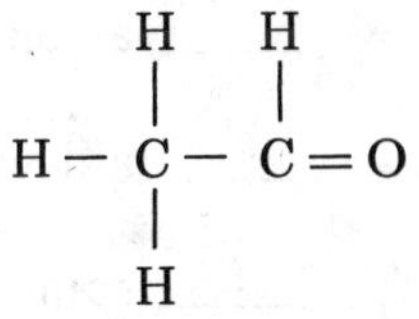

____ alcohol

✓ aldehyde

____ some other type

Why? Because it has a CHO group

---

aldehyde; It has a CHO group. (or equivalent answer)

192.

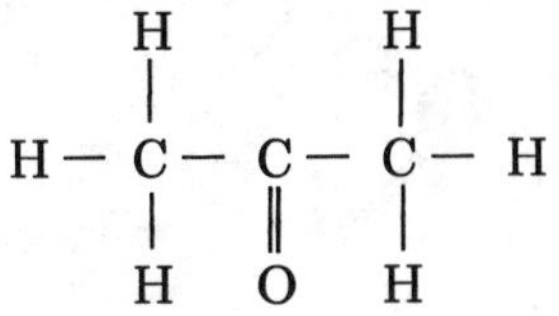

____ alcohol

____ aldehyde

✓ some other type

Why? ~~It~~ has neither —OH nor CHO

---

some other type; It has neither an —OH group nor a CHO group.

193.

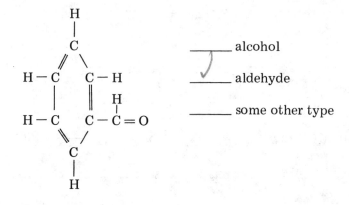

H
|
C
// \
H — C   C — H
| ||
| H
| |
H — C   C — C = O
\\ /
C
|
H

_____ alcohol

__✓__ aldehyde

_____ some other type

Why? _____It has a CHO group_____

_____

aldehyde; It has a CHO group.

194.

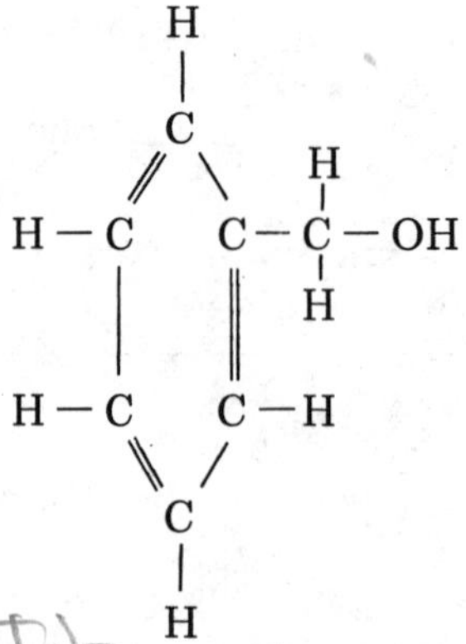

H
|
C
// \   H
H — C   C — C — OH
| |
| H
|
H — C   C — H
\\ /
C
|
H

_____ alcohol

_____ aldehyde

_____ some other type

Why? _____It has an —OH group_____

_____

alcohol; It has an —OH group.

195. $CH_3CH_2CH_2CH_2OH$ ___✓___ alcohol

                                                        _____ aldehyde

                                                        _____ some other type

Why? __It has an —OH group__

_____

alcohol; It has an —OH group.

196. 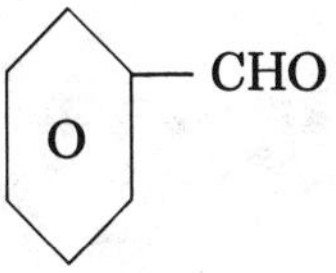   _____ alcohol
         ⬡—CHO   ___✓___ aldehyde
         O
                                               _____ some other type

Why? ___It has CHO_____

_____

aldehyde; It has a CHO group.

197.

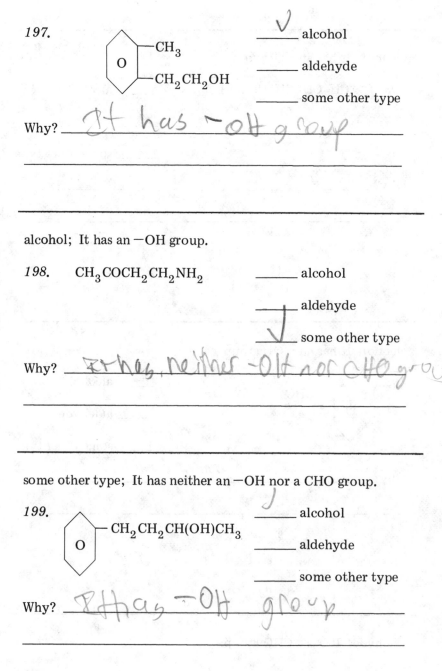

―CH$_3$

O

―CH$_2$CH$_2$OH

_____ alcohol

_____ aldehyde

_____ some other type

Why? _It has ―OH group_

_____

alcohol; It has an ―OH group.

198.   CH$_3$COCH$_2$CH$_2$NH$_2$

_____ alcohol

_____ aldehyde

_____ some other type

Why? _It has neither ―OH nor CHO group_

_____

some other type; It has neither an ―OH nor a CHO group.

199.

―CH$_2$CH$_2$CH(OH)CH$_3$

O

_____ alcohol

_____ aldehyde

_____ some other type

Why? _It has ―OH group_

_____

84

alcohol; It has an −OH group.

200. A compound that contains the following group is called a *ketone*.

$$C - C - C$$
$$\overset{\shortparallel}{O}$$

Note that the ketone group contains a carbon atom attached to a double-bonded oxygen atom, and is between two other carbon atoms.

201. a.   An alcohol contains the ___OH___ group.

b.   An aldehyde contains the ___CHO___ group.

c.   A ketone contains the ___C−C−C / O___ group.

a.   OH;   b.   CHO;   c.   C−C−C
$$\overset{\shortparallel}{O}$$

Identify the compounds in the next ten frames as alcohols, aldehydes, or ketones.

202.

$$H - \overset{\displaystyle H}{\underset{\displaystyle H}{C}} - \overset{\displaystyle H}{\underset{\displaystyle H}{C}} - \overset{\displaystyle H}{\underset{\displaystyle H}{C}} - \overset{\displaystyle H}{\underset{\displaystyle OH}{C}} - \overset{\displaystyle H}{\underset{\displaystyle H}{C}} - H$$

___✓___ alcohol

_____ aldehyde

_____ ketone

85

alcohol

203.

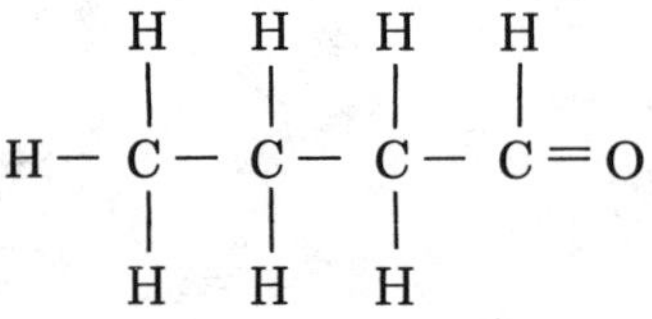

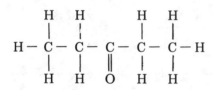

H $-$ C $-$ C $-$ C $-$ C $=$ O

_____ alcohol

✓_____ aldehyde

_____ ketone

aldehyde

204.

H $-$ C $-$ C $-$ C $-$ C $-$ C $-$ H

_____ alcohol

_____ aldehyde

✓_____ ketone

ketone

205.

$CH_3 CH(OH)CH_3$

✓_____ alcohol

_____ aldehyde

_____ ketone

alcohol

206.

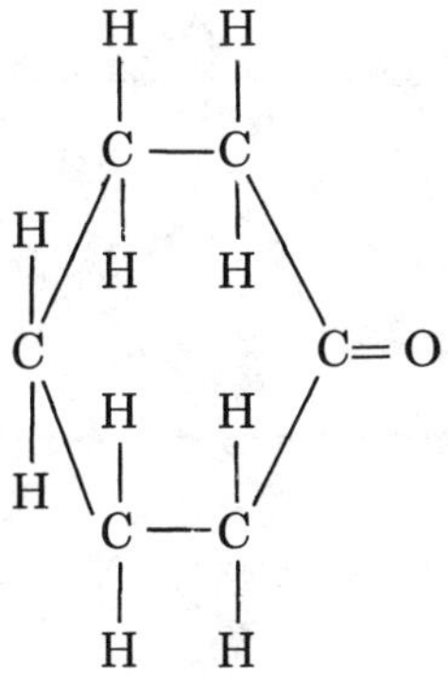

_____ alcohol

_____ aldehyde

✓ ketone

---

ketone

207.

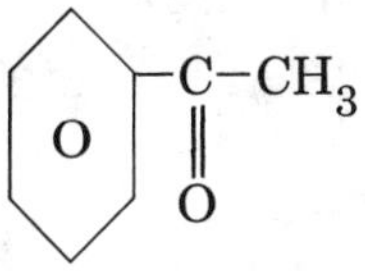

_____ alcohol

_____ aldehyde

✓ ketone

---

ketone

208.

$CH_3 C - CH_2 - CH_2 CHO$
            $\|$
            O

_____ alcohol and ketone

✓ aldehyde and ketone

_____ alcohol and aldehyde

---

aldehyde and ketone

209.

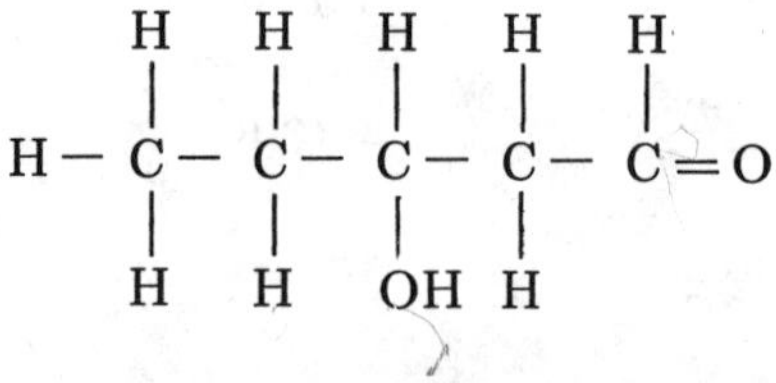

```
        H    H    H    H    H
        |    |    |    |    |
  H  —  C  — C  — C  — C  — C = O
        |    |    |    |
        H    H    OH   H
```

aldehyde + alcohol

---

alcohol and aldehyde

210.

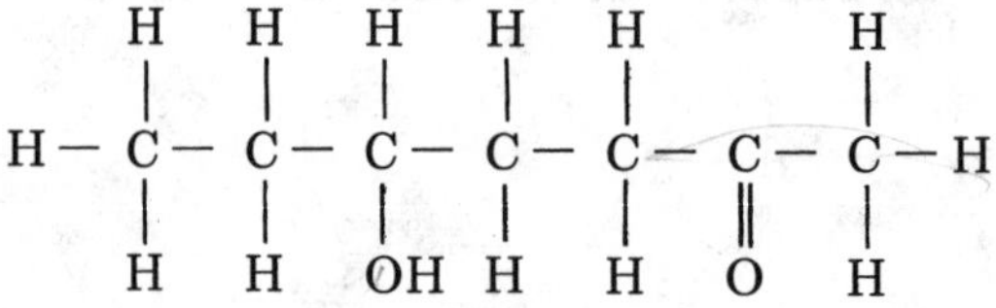

ketone + alcohol

```
        H    H    H    H    H         H
        |    |    |    |    |         |
  H  —  C  — C  — C  — C  — C  — C  — C — H
        |    |    |    |    |    ||    |
        H    H    OH   H    H    O     H
```

---

ketone and alcohol

211.

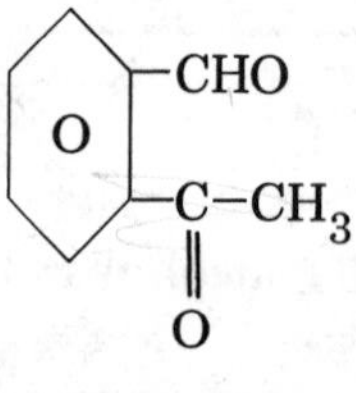

ketone + aldehyde

---

aldehyde and ketone

212. A compound that contains a COOH group is called an acid.

The COOH group may also be written as

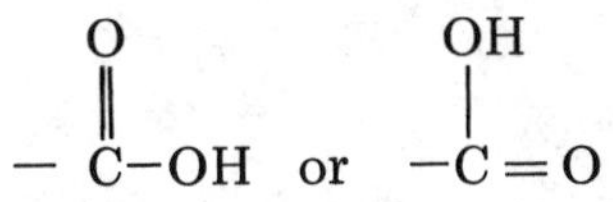

$$\begin{matrix} O \\ \parallel \\ -\ C-OH \end{matrix} \quad or \quad \begin{matrix} OH \\ \vert \\ -C=O \end{matrix}$$

A compound with a CHO group is called _aldehyde_.

A compound with a COOH group is called _acid_.

---

an aldehyde; an acid

213. A compound with an OH group is called _alcohol_.

A compound with a C—C—C group is called _ketone_.
$\qquad\qquad\qquad\qquad\quad\ \ \begin{matrix}\ \ \vert\!\vert \\ \ \ O\end{matrix}$

---

an alcohol; a ketone

214. A compound that contains an NH_2 group is called an *amine*.

In the NH_2 group,

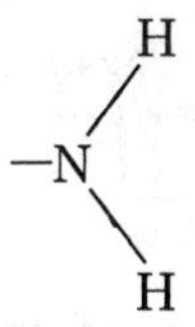

$$-N\begin{matrix} \diagup H \\ \diagdown H \end{matrix}$$

89

the nitrogen atoms has 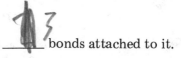 bonds attached to it.

3

215. a.   An organic acid is a compound containing a _COOH_ group.

b.   A compound containing an NH_2 group is called _amine_ _____.

c.   A compound containing an OH group is called _an alcohol_ _____.

d.   A compound containing a CHO group is called _an aldehyde_ _____.

e.   A compound containing a C–C–C group is called _____
ketone _____.
$$\underset{O}{\overset{\parallel}{}}$$

---

a.   COOH;   b. an amine;   c. an alcohol;   d. an aldehyde;
e.   a ketone

*Identify the types of compounds in the next five frames. Write
the reasons for your choices on the lines provided.*

216.
$$H - \underset{\underset{H}{|}}{\overset{\overset{H}{|}}{C}} - \underset{\underset{NH_2}{|}}{\overset{\overset{H}{|}}{C}} - \underset{\underset{H}{|}}{\overset{\overset{H}{|}}{C}} - H$$

_____ alcohol
__✓__ amine
_____ ketone
_____ aldehyde
_____ acid

Why?   _It has a NH_2 group_

amine; It contains an NH$_2$ group.

217.

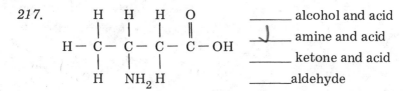

           _____ alcohol and acid

           __√__ amine and acid

           _____ ketone and acid

           _____aldehyde

Why? It has a NH$_2$ group and a COOH group

---

amine and acid, or amino acid; It contains both NH$_2$ and COOH groups.

218.

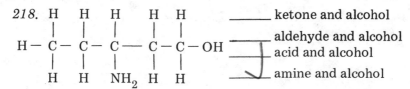

           _____ ketone and alcohol

           _____ aldehyde and alcohol

           _____ acid and alcohol

           __√__ amine and alcohol

Why? It has a NH$_2$ and OH group

---

amine and alcohol, or amino alcohol; It contains both NH$_2$ and OH groups.

91

219.

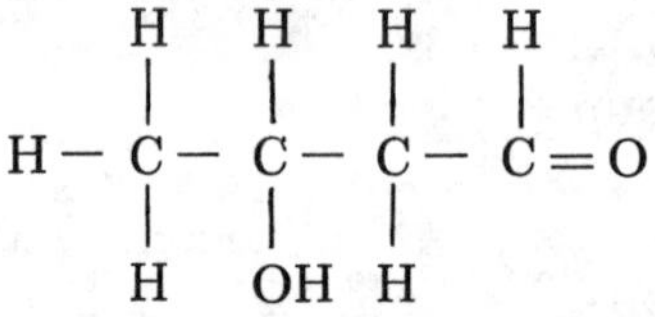

H − C − C − C − C = O

with H H H H on top, and H OH H below (structure of compound)

_____ alcohol and acid
_____ amine and alcohol
__✓__ alcohol and aldehyde
_____ ketone and alcohol

Why? _It has a CHO group and OH_

alcohol and aldehyde; It contains both CHO and OH groups.

220.

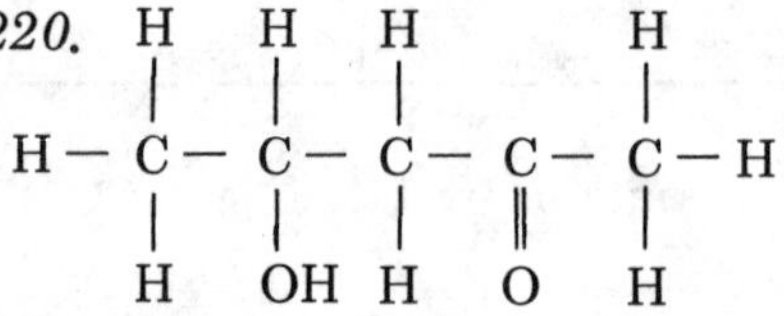

H − C − C − C − C − C − H

with H H H H on top, and H OH H O H below (structure of compound)

_____ amine and alcohol
_____ acid and alcohol
_____ alcohol and aldehyde
__✓__ alcohol and ketone

Why? _It has OH and C−C−C (with double bond O)_

alcohol and ketone; It contains both OH and C—C—C groups.

$$\overset{\|}{O}$$

Identify the compounds given in the next five frames as to type.

92

221.

COOH

alcohol + acid

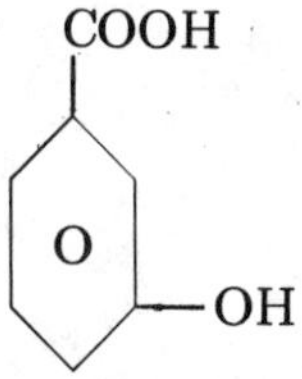

---

acid and alcohol

222.

$$CH_3CH(NH_2)COOH$$

Amino acid

---

amine and acid (amino acid)

223.

$$CH_3C-CH_2CH_2NH_2$$
$$\parallel$$
$$O$$

ketone amine

---

ketone and amine

224.

$$CH_3CH_2CH(OH)COOH$$

Alcohol + acid

---

alcohol and acid

93

225. $\text{\itshape aldehyde + amine}$ *aldehyde + amine* (handwritten)

---

aldehyde and amine

226. A compound that contains a COOC group is called an *ester*.
This group may also be written as

$$\overset{\displaystyle O}{\overset{\|}{C}} - O - C \quad \text{or} \quad \overset{\displaystyle C}{\underset{\displaystyle C=O}{\overset{|}{\underset{|}{O}}}} \quad \text{or} \quad C-O-C=O \quad \text{or} \quad C-O-\overset{\displaystyle O}{\overset{\|}{C}}$$

The following compound is an ester because it contains a COOC
group:

$$H - \overset{\displaystyle H}{\underset{\displaystyle H}{\overset{|}{\underset{|}{C}}}} - \overset{\displaystyle O}{\overset{\|}{C}} - O - \overset{\displaystyle H}{\underset{\displaystyle H}{\overset{|}{\underset{|}{C}}}} - H$$

227. A compound that contains a $-OPO_3H_2$ group is called a
phosphate. This group may also be written as

$$-O - \overset{\displaystyle O}{\underset{\displaystyle OH}{\overset{\|}{\underset{|}{P}}}} - OH$$

94

The following compound is a phosphate because it contains the $-OPO_3H_2$ group:

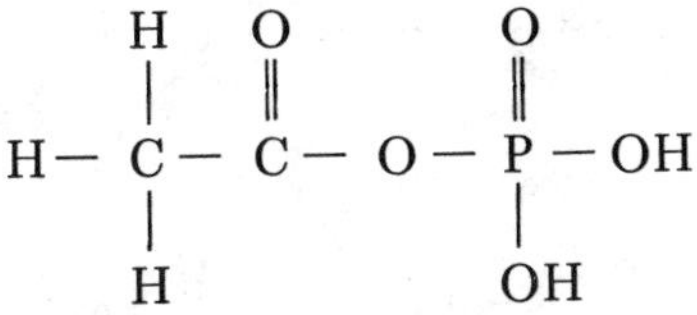

$$H-\overset{\overset{\displaystyle H}{|}}{\underset{\underset{\displaystyle H}{|}}{C}}-\overset{\overset{\displaystyle O}{\|}}{C}-O-\overset{\overset{\displaystyle O}{\|}}{\underset{\underset{\displaystyle OH}{|}}{P}}-OH$$

228. The following compound is what type?

$\qquad\qquad\qquad\qquad$ *ester*

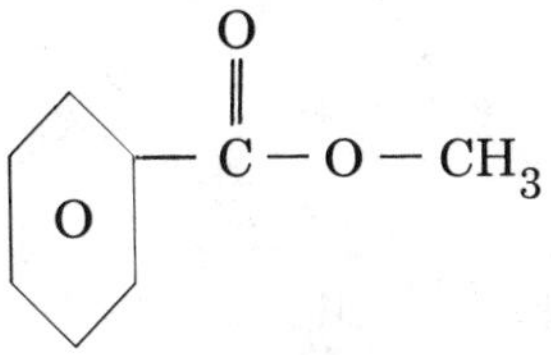

$$\text{(benzene ring)}-\overset{\overset{\displaystyle O}{\|}}{C}-O-CH_3$$

_____

ester

229. The following structure represents adenosine monophosphate (AMP):

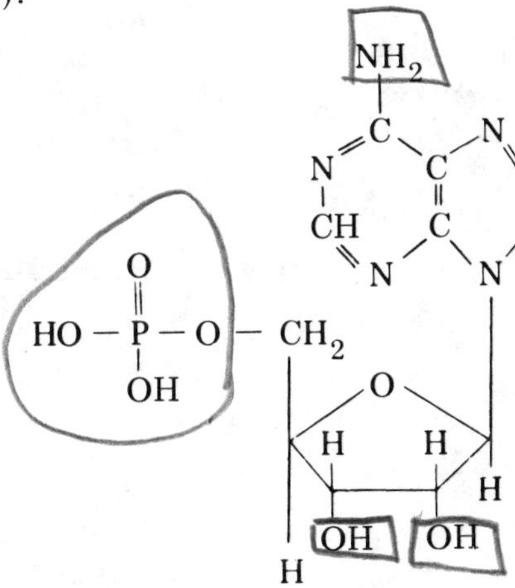

Draw a circle around the phosphate group. This compound also contains an amine and two alcohol groups. Draw a square around the amine group, and a rectangle around the OH groups.

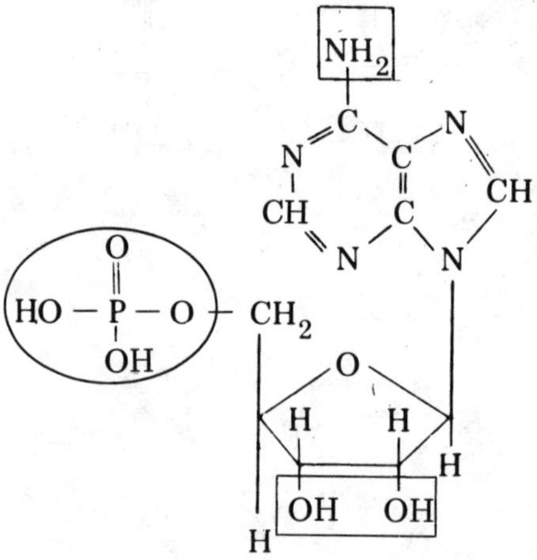

Summary of Functional Groups

Indicate the formula and the name of each of the functional groups following, as in the first example.

230.   (group) _____ OH _____

                                  (name) _____ alcohol _____

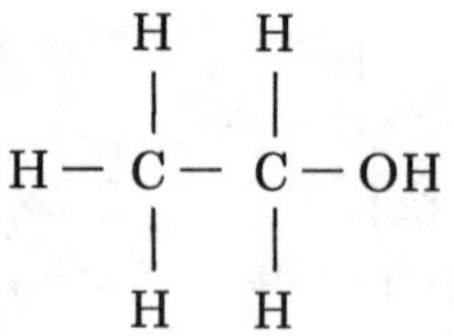

231.

(group) COOH

(name) acid

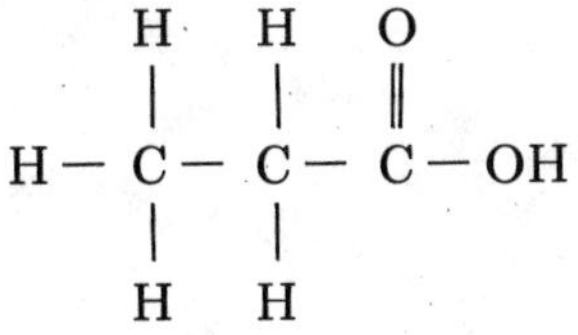

```
        H   H   O
        |   |   ‖
  H —  C — C — C — OH
        |   |
        H   H
```

COOH; acid

232.

(group) COOC

(name) ester

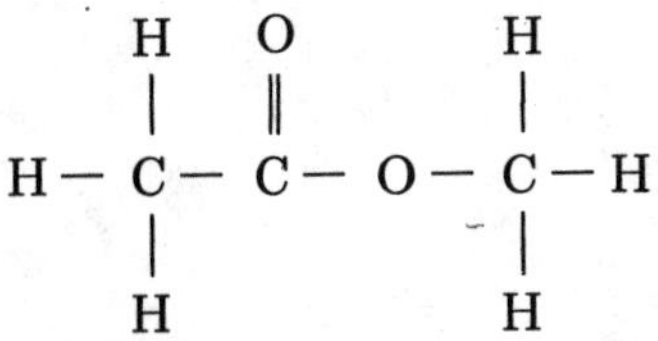

```
        H   O           H
        |   ‖           |
  H —  C — C — O —  C — H
        |               |
        H               H
```

COOC; ester

233.

(group) C—C—C ‖ O

(name) Ketone

```
        H           H
        |           |
  H —  C — C —  C — H
        |   ‖       |
        H   O       H
```

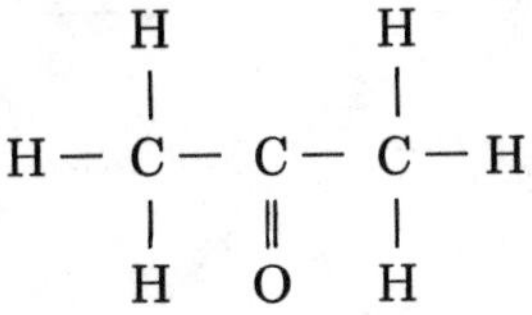

C–C–C; ketone
 ‖
 O

234.

(group) NH₂

(name) amine

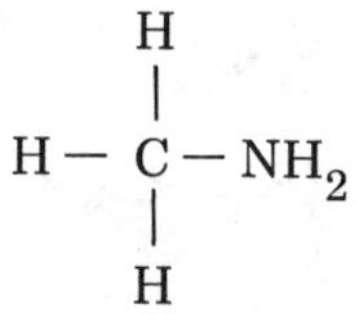

$$H - \overset{\overset{\displaystyle H}{|}}{\underset{\underset{\displaystyle H}{|}}{C}} - NH_2$$

NH_2; amine

235.

(group) CHO

(name) aldehyde

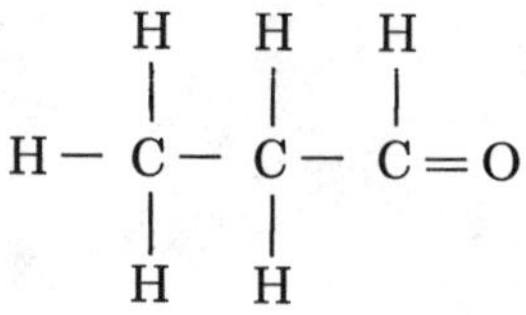

$$H - \overset{\overset{\displaystyle H}{|}}{\underset{\underset{\displaystyle H}{|}}{C}} - \overset{\overset{\displaystyle H}{|}}{\underset{\underset{\displaystyle H}{|}}{C}} - \overset{\overset{\displaystyle H}{|}}{C} = O$$

CHO; aldehyde

236.

(group) NH₂

(name) amine

 — NH₂

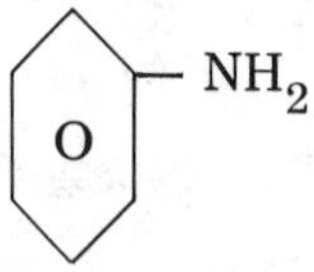

NH_2; amine

98

237.   (group) $-OPO_3H_2$

                              (name) *phosphate*

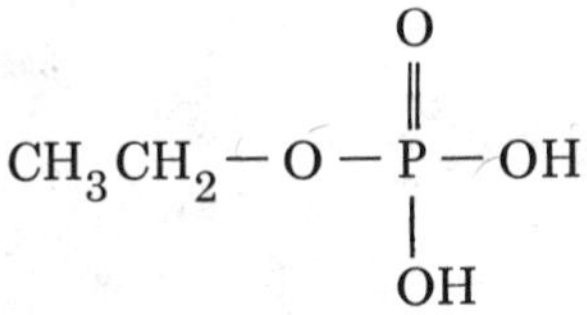

$$CH_3CH_2-O-\overset{\overset{\textstyle O}{\|}}{\underset{\underset{\textstyle OH}{|}}{P}}-OH$$

$-OPO_3H_2$; phosphate

238.   (group) $C-\underset{\underset{\textstyle O}{}}{C}-C$

                              (name) *ketone*

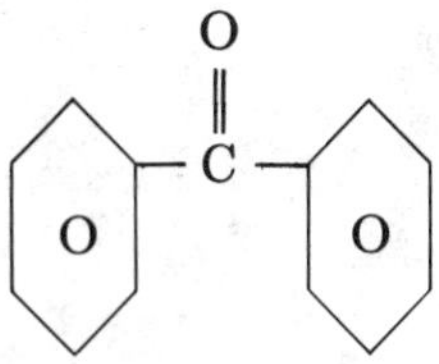

C–C–C; ketone
$\overset{\|}{O}$

239.   (group) OH

                              (name) *alcohol*

$$CH_3CH(OH)CH_3$$

$-OH$; alcohol

240.
(group) _COOC_

(name) _ester_

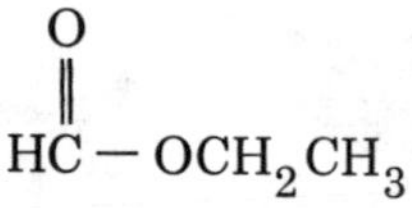

$$\overset{\displaystyle O}{\underset{\displaystyle \|}{HC}} - OCH_2CH_3$$

COOC; ester

Name the groups present in the following compounds.

241.

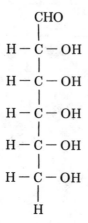

$$CHO$$
$$H - C - OH$$
$$H - C - OH$$
$$H - C - OH$$
$$H - C - OH$$
$$H - C - OH$$
$$H$$

aldehydes

alcohols

---

aldehyde and alcohols (more than one alcohol group)

242.

amines

acid

$$CH_3CH_2CH(NH_2)COOH$$

---

amine and acid (amino acid)

100

243.

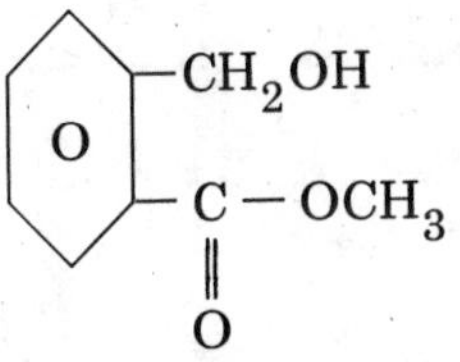

ester

alcohol

alcohol and ester

244.

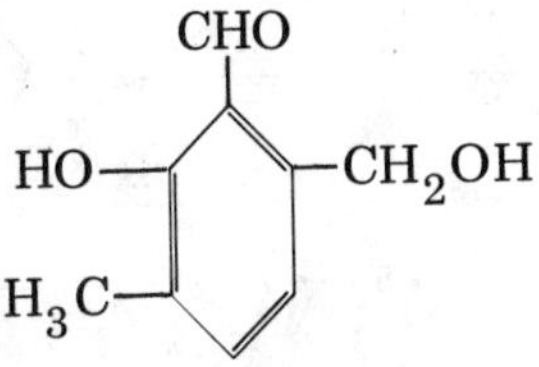

aldehyde

alcohol.

Pyridoxal, one of the B vitamins

aldehyde and alcohols

245.

ester

phosphate

$C_{17}H_{35}COO\text{-}CH_2$

$C_{17}H_{35}COO\text{-}CH$

$H_2O_3PO\text{—}CH_2$

Fat

one phosphate group and two ester groups

246.

O
‖
⬡ — CH=... COOH

OH   OH

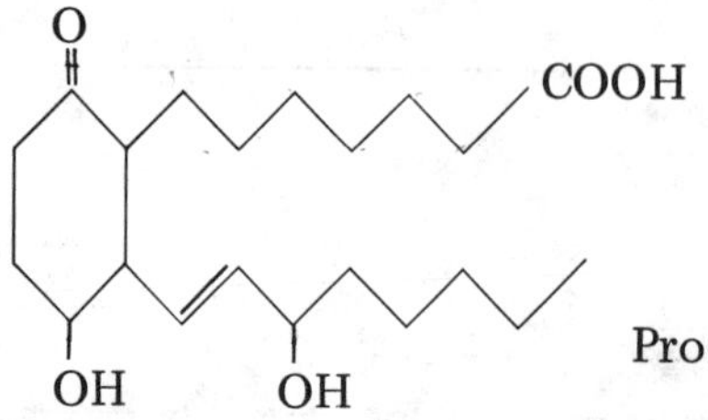

Prostaglandin

---

two alcohol groups, a ketone group, and an acid group

247.

$COOH$
|
$CHNH_2$
|
CH_2OH

Serine

---

an alcohol, an amine, and an acid group

248.

CHO
|
$HC-OH$
|
$H_2C-OPO_3H_2$

---

aldehyde, alcohol, and phosphate groups

102

249.

$$CH_2 - O\overset{\overset{\displaystyle O}{\|}}{C} - C_{17}H_{35}$$

$$CH - O - \overset{\overset{\displaystyle O}{\|}}{C} - C_{17}H_{35}$$

$$CH_2 - O\underset{\underset{\displaystyle OH}{|}}{\overset{\overset{\displaystyle O}{\|}}{P}} - OCH_2CH_2NH_2$$

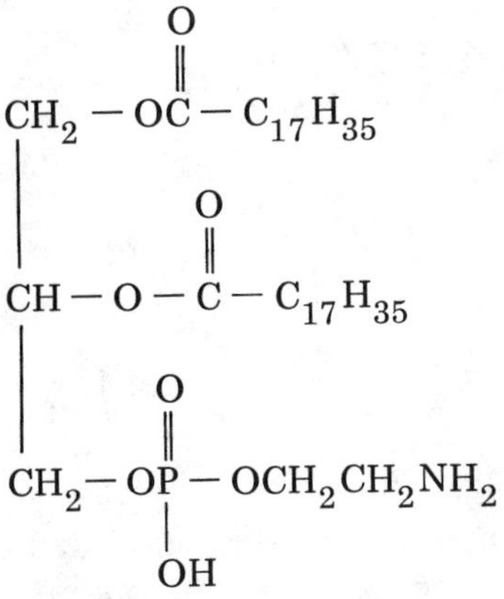

Cephalin

---

two ester groups, a phosphate group, and an amine group

IV
CARBOHYDRATES, FATS, PROTEIN

250. Carbohydrates contain the elements carbon, hydrogen, and oxygen, and only those elements. A compound containing elements other than those three is not a carbohydrate.

The word *hydrate* refers to water. Carbohydrates usually contain hydrogen and oxygen in the same ratio as in water—2:1.

Which of the following compounds are carbohydrates?

    a. C_6H_6 d. $C_6H_{12}O_6N$

    b. $C_{12}H_{22}O_{11}$ e. C_2H_6O

    c. $C_5H_{10}O_5$

---

b. $C_{12}H_{22}O_{11}$ and c. $C_5H_{10}O_5$

251. In the list of compounds above, why is $C_6H_{12}O_6N$ not a carbohydrate? because it contains

nitrogen

Why are C_6H_6 and C_2H_6O not carbohydrates? _becqdse_

C₆H₆ has no Oxygen and C₂H₆O
does not have twice as much H as O

$C_6H_{12}O_6N$ contains nitrogen, and carbohydrates contain only C, H, and O. C_6H_6 contains no oxygen, and C_6H_6O has the wrong ratio of H to O.

252. Carbohydrates are divided into three types. One type of carbohydrate is the *monosaccharide*. The chief function of monosaccharides in the body is to provide energy.

The word *saccharide* means *simple sugar*. The prefix *mono* means __One__.

Therefore, monosaccharides are simple sugars, each containing only __one__ simple sugar.

---

one; one

253. Monosaccharides are named for the number of carbon atoms they contain. The most common monosaccharides contain *six* carbon atoms, so they are called *hexoses*.

Three common hexoses are *glucose*, *galactose*, and *fructose*. They all contain __six__ carbon atoms.

---

six

254. Glucose, galactose, and fructose, the three common hexoses, all have the same molecular formula, $C_6H_{12}O_6$. Their structural formulas are given below:

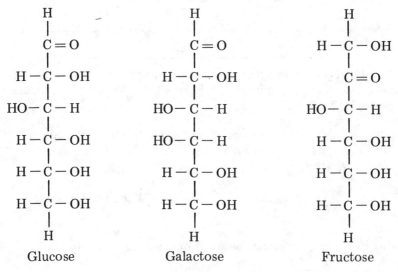

| Glucose | Galactose | Fructose |

Look at the structures of the above three hexoses. They all have the same molecular formula (count them), ~~$C_6H_{12}O_6$~~ .

$C_6H_{12}O_6$

255. Glucose contains what two types of functional groups? ~~alcohol , aldehyde~~

---

alcohol and aldehyde

256. Galactose contains what groups? ~~alcohol,~~
~~aldehyde~~

alcohol and aldehyde

257. Fructose contains what two types of groups? _alcohol_
ketone

---

alcohol and ketone

258. Monosaccharides containing six carbon atoms are called
hexoses.

---

hexoses

259. The three common monosaccharides are galactose, fructose,
and _glucose_.

---

glucose

260. The second type of carbohydrate is called the *disaccharide*.
The prefix *di* means *two*.

Disaccharides are formed by the combination of two monosaccharides, with water also being produced.

monosaccharide + monosaccharide ⟶ disaccharide + water

Conversely, disaccharides react with water to produce two monosaccharides.

disaccharide + water ⟶ monosaccharide + _monosaccharide_

monosaccharide

261. This reaction (a reaction with water) is called *hydrolysis.*

Disaccharides, on hydrolysis, yield two _monosaccharides_

---

monosaccharides

262. Monosaccharides contain ___/___ simple sugar(s).
Disaccharides contain ___2___ simple sugar(s).

---

one; two

263. The hydrolysis of a disaccharide may be written as:

$$C_{12}H_{22}O_{11} + H_2O \longrightarrow C_6H_{12}O_6 + C_6H_{12}O_6$$
disaccharide + water   monosaccharide + monosaccharide

Sucrose, $C_{12}H_{22}O_{11}$, is a disaccharide. The hydrolysis of
sucrose yields the two _monosaccharides_ glucose and
fructose.

---

monosaccharides.

264. There are three common disaccharides: *sucrose, maltose,*
and *lactose.* These disaccharides all have the same molecular
formula, $C_{12}H_{22}O_{11}$.

Lactose, also called milk sugar, is found in milk.

Maltose, or malt sugar, is found in sprouting grain.

Sucrose, or cane sugar, is found in _sugar cane_.

---

sugar cane

265. Three monosaccharides are _glucose_,
fructose, and _galactose_.

Sucrose, _maltose_, and lactose are disaccharides.

---

glucose, fructose, galactose (any order); maltose

266. The third type of carbohydrate is the *polysaccharide*.

The prefix *poly* means *many*, so polysaccharides, on hydrolysis,
yield many _mono saccharides_

---

monosaccharides

267. Starch is a polysaccharide. Its molecular formula is
$(C_6H_{10}O_5)_n$, where n is some large number. Upon complete
hydrolysis, starch yields many monosaccharides.

$$(C_6H_{10}O_5)_n + nH_2O \longrightarrow nC_6H_{12}O_6$$

starch,
a polysaccharide   monosaccharides

Which of the following formulas represents a disaccharide?

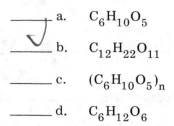

    a. $C_6H_{10}O_5$

    b. $C_{12}H_{22}O_{11}$

    c. $(C_6H_{10}O_5)_n$

    d. $C_6H_{12}O_6$

---

b. $C_{12}H_{22}O_{11}$

268. Which of the formulas listed in frame 267 represents a polysaccharide? _____ $(C_6H_{10}O_5)_n$ _____

Which are monosaccharides? _____ $C_6H_{12}O_6$, $C_6H_{10}O_5$ _____

---

c. $(C_6H_{10}O_5)_n$

a. $C_6H_{10}O_5$ and d. $C_6H_{12}O_6$

269. Other examples of polysaccharides are *cellulose*, found in plants, and *glycogen*, found in animals. Plants use the poly-saccharide cellulose primarily for support. Animals store carbo-hydrate in the form of a polysaccharide, glycogen.

a.   Name three common monosaccharides. galactose , glucose , fructose

b.   Name three common disaccharides. sucrose , lactose , maltose

c.   Name three polysaccharides. _Starch_____,
_____cellulose_____, ____glucogen_____

---

a.   glucose, fructose, galactose;   b.   lactose, maltose, sucrose
c.   starch, cellulose, glycogen

270. Carbohydrates contain the elements _Carbon_____,
_____Hydrogen_____, and ____Oxygen_____.

---

carbon, hydrogen, oxygen

271. Fats contain the same elements as do carbohydrates, but
with less oxygen in proportion than carbohydrates.

Upon hydrolysis, fats yield *fatty acids* and *glycerol*, an alcohol.
Glycerol is also known as *glycerin.*

The hydrolysis of a fat may be written as:

$$\text{fat} \xrightarrow{\text{(hydrolysis)}} \text{fatty acids} + \text{glycerol}$$

Remember, hydrolysis means *reaction with* ___water___.

---

water

272. Fatty acids and glycerol are products of the hydrolysis of
a ___fat___.

fat

273. Complete the following equation:

fat + water $\xrightarrow{\text{(hydrolysis)}}$ _fatty acids_ + _glycerol_

---

fatty acids + glycerol

274. The chemical equation for the hydrolysis of a fat may be written as

$$
\begin{array}{c}
\text{H} \quad\; \text{O} \\
| \qquad || \\
\text{H–C–O–C–C}_{17}\text{H}_{35} \\
| \\
\quad\;\;\; \text{O} \\
\quad\;\;\; || \\
\text{H–C–O–C–C}_{17}\text{H}_{35} \\
| \\
\quad\;\;\; \text{O} \\
\quad\;\;\; || \\
\text{H–C–O–C–C}_{17}\text{H}_{35} \\
| \\
\text{H}
\end{array}
\; + \; 3\text{H}_2\text{O} \longrightarrow 3\text{C}_{17}\text{H}_{35}\text{COOH} +
\begin{array}{c}
\text{H} \\
| \\
\text{H–C–OH} \\
| \\
\text{H–C–OH} \\
| \\
\text{H–C–OH} \\
| \\
\text{H}
\end{array}
$$

|⎣_____A_____⎦|⎣_____B_____⎦|⎣__C__⎦|

Substance A is a fat.
Substance B is a ___fatty acid___.
Substance C is an alcohol called ___glycerol___.
Substance A contains what type of groups? ___esters___.

112

fatty acid; glycerol; esters

275. How do you know substance B is an acid? _because_
it has COOH .

How do you know substance C is an alcohol? _because_
it has −OH .

Why is substance A called an ester? _because it has COOC_
 .

It contains COOH groups.
It contains −OH groups.
It contains O   O   groups.
          ‖   ‖
       C−O−C (C−O−C)

276. a. The hydrolysis of a polysaccharide yields _many_
monosaccharides

b. The hydrolysis of a disaccharide yields _2 monosaccharides_
 .

c. The hydrolysis of a fat yields _fatty acids and_
glycerol .

---

a. many monosaccharides;   b. two monosaccharides;
c. fatty acids and glycerol

Proteins

277. Proteins contain the same elements as do carbohydrates and fats, except that proteins *always* contain one additional element—nitrogen.

All proteins contain the four elements:

1. _carbon_   3. _oxygen_
2. _nitrogen_   4. _hydrogen_

---

carbon; hydrogen; oxygen; nitrogen (in any order)

278. Some proteins also contain additional elements, such as sulfur, phosphorus, or iron.

The hydrolysis of proteins yields *amino acids.*

Amino acids contain what functional groups? _amines_ _acids_

---

amine and acid (or NH_2 and COOH)

279. The hydrolysis of proteins yields amino acids. Likewise, the combination of amino acids yields proteins.

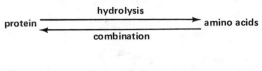

protein $\xrightarrow{\text{hydrolysis}}$ amino acids

combination

280. When two amino acids combine, the product is called a *dipeptide*.

A *tripeptide* would be formed when ___3___ amino acids combined.

A *polypeptide* would be formed when __many__ amino acids combined.

3; many (or more than 3)

281. Notice the formulas for alanine and glycine indicated below:

$$CH_3 - CH - COOH \qquad CH_2COOH$$
$$\quad\quad | \qquad\qquad\qquad\quad |$$
$$\quad\quad NH_2 \qquad\qquad\qquad NH_2$$

Alanine   Glycine

Both would be classified as what type of compounds? __amino acids__

---

amino acids

282. When these two amino acids react, the following reactions are possible:

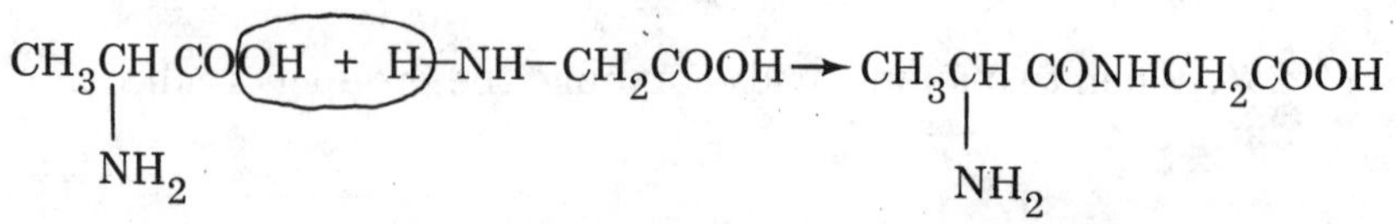

$$CH_3CH\ CO\!\boxed{OH}\ +\ H\!\!-\!\!NH\!-\!CH_2COOH \rightarrow CH_3CH\ CONHCH_2COOH$$

$$\underset{NH_2}{|} \qquad\qquad\qquad\qquad\qquad\qquad \underset{NH_2}{|}$$

alanine   glycine   alanyl-glycine (ala-gly)

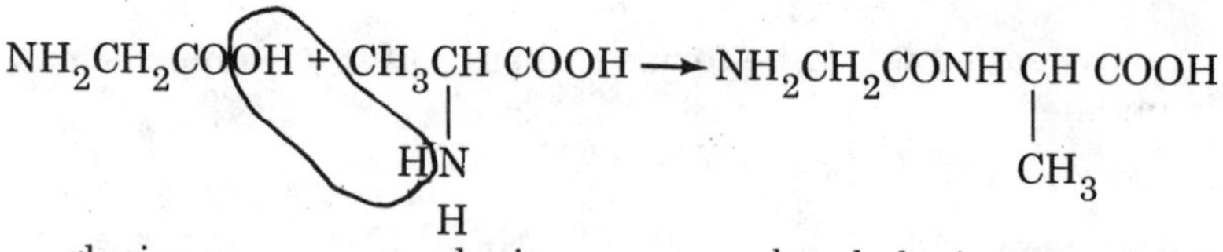

$$NH_2CH_2CO\!\boxed{OH}\ +\ CH_3CH\ COOH \rightarrow NH_2CH_2CONH\ CH\ COOH$$

$$\qquad\qquad\qquad \underset{\underset{H}{HN}}{|} \qquad\qquad\qquad\qquad \underset{CH_3}{|}$$

glycine   alanine   glycyl-alanine (gly-ala)

Note that in both of these equations, the reaction is between the OH of a(n) ___acid___ group and the H of a(n) ___amine___ group.

___

acid; amine

283. When these two amino acids react, what type of compound is formed? ___dipeptide___

___

a dipeptide

284. The abbreviation *ala* represents ___alanine___.

The abbreviation *ala-gly* represents ___alanyl-glycine___

---

alanine; alanyl-glycine

285. If the amino acids glycine, alanine, and valine were combined in one compound, what type would it be? ___tripeptide___
_____.

---

a tripeptide

286. What would be the abbreviation for a tripeptide containing alanine, glycine and valine, in that order? ___ala-gly-val___

---

ala-gly-val

287. What would the abbreviation *gly-val-ala* represent?
___glycyl-valanyl-alanine___

---

a tripeptide containing glycine, valine, and alanine, combined in that order

Oxidation-Reduction

288. Oxidation may be defined as either *the loss of hydrogen by a compound* or *the gain of oxygen by a compound.*

The compound *lactic acid* may be oxidized to *pyruvic acid* according to the following equation.

Lactic acid   Pyruvic acid

This is an oxidation reaction because it involves: (check one)

     _____ the gain of oxygen by the lactic acid molecule
     ___✓___ the loss of hydrogen by the lactic acid molecule

---

the loss of hydrogen by the lactic acid molecule

289. Lactic acid contains what functional groups?
   alcohol, acid

Pyruvic acid contains what functional groups?
   ketone, acid

---

alcohol and acid; ketone and acid

118

290. Similarly, succinic acid may be oxidized to fumaric acid.

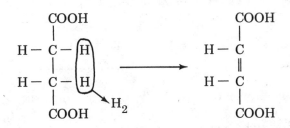

Succinic acid   Fumaric acid

This is an oxidation reaction because it involves *He loss of hydrogen* .

---

loss of hydrogen

291. Another example of oxidation is the reaction of acetalde-hyde to form acetic acid.

$$H - \overset{\overset{\displaystyle H}{|}}{\underset{\underset{\displaystyle H}{|}}{C}} - \overset{\displaystyle H}{C} = O \longrightarrow H - \overset{\overset{\displaystyle H}{|}}{\underset{\underset{\displaystyle H}{|}}{C}} - \overset{\displaystyle OH}{C} = O$$

Acetaldehyde   Acetic acid

This reaction is oxidation because it involves *gain of oxygen* .

---

gain of oxygen

292. *Reduction* is the reverse of oxidation. Oxidation is the loss of hydrogen or the gain of oxygen by a compound. Therefore, reduction is *gain of hydrogen or loss of oxygen*

---

the gain of hydrogen or loss of oxygen by a compound

293. An oil may be changed to a fat by a process of reduction. This process involves the addition of hydrogen to the oil.

$$\text{oil} \xrightarrow{\quad\text{(hydrogen)}\quad} \text{fat}$$

Oxidation is *loss of hydrogen of gain of oxygen*

Reduction is *gain of hydrogen or loss of oxygen*

---

the loss of hydrogen or the gain of oxygen
the gain of hydrogen or the loss of oxygen

294. An example of a reduction reaction is that of benzaldehyde to benzyl alcohol.

Benzaldehyde   Benzyl alcohol

This is a reduction reaction because it involves *gain of hydrogen*.

120

the gain of hydrogen

295. Another example of a reduction reaction is that of acetic acid to acetaldehyde.

$$CH_3COOH \longrightarrow CH_3CHO$$

Acetic acid   Acetaldehyde

This is a reduction reaction because it involves <u>loss of</u> <u>oxygen</u>.

---

loss of oxygen

Are the reactions in the following frames oxidation or reduction? Why?

296.

$$
\begin{array}{ccc}
\text{COOH} & & \text{COOH} \\
| & & | \\
\text{H} - \text{C} - \text{OH} & & \text{C} = \text{O} \\
| & \longrightarrow & | \\
\text{H} - \text{C} - \text{H} & & \text{H} - \text{C} - \text{H} \\
| & & | \\
\text{COOH} & & \text{COOH}
\end{array}
$$

Maleic acid   Oxaloacetic acid

Reaction: <u>oxidation</u>
Why? <u>loss of hydrogen</u>

---

oxidation; loss of hydrogen

121

297.

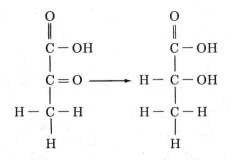

Pyruvic acid   Lactic acid

Reaction: _reduction_

Why? _gain of H_

---

reduction; gain of hydrogen

298.

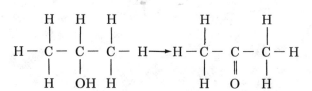

Isopropyl alcohol   Acetone

Reaction: _oxidation_

Why? _loss of H_

---

oxidation; loss of hydrogen

299. $CH_3COCH_2COOH \longrightarrow CH_3CH(OH)CH_2COOH$

Acetoacetic acid β-hydroxybutyric acid

Reaction: *reduction*
Why? *gain of hydrogen*

---

reduction; gain of hydrogen

300.

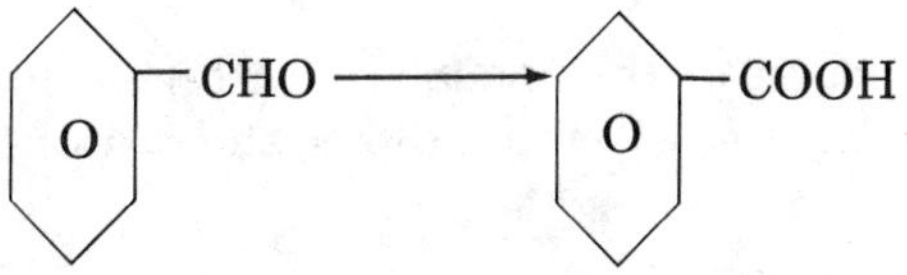

Benzaldehyde   Benzoic acid

Reaction: *oxidation*
Why? *gain of oxygen*

---

oxidation; gain of oxygen

301. CH_2OH CH_2OH

$HO-C-H \longrightarrow C=O$

$CH_2OPO_3H_2$ $CH_2OPO_3H_2$

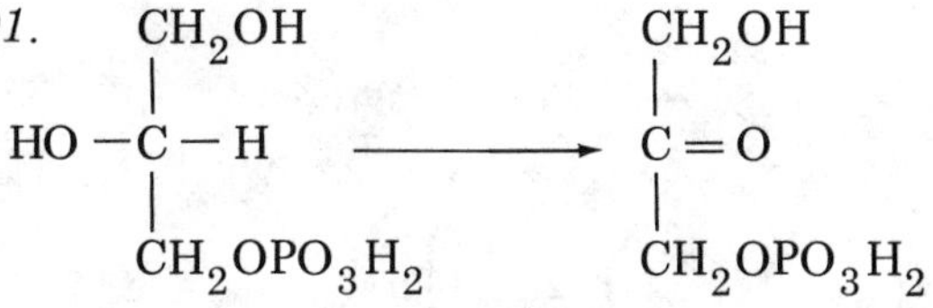

2 - glycerophosphate   Dihydroxyacetone phosphate

Reaction: *oxidation*
Why? *loss of H*

oxidation; loss of hydrogen

Review

302. Diagram the structure of the phosphorus atom, atomic number 15 and mass number 31, and indicate the protons, neutrons, and electrons in each energy level.

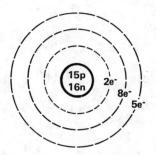

303. Diagram the structures of two isotopes of sodium, atomic number 11 and mass numbers 23 and 24.

124

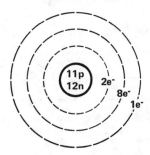 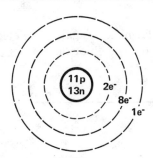

304. What elements do the following symbols represent?

H _Hydrogen_   O _Oxygen_

S _Sulfur_   Na _Sodium_

K _Potassium_   Fe _Iron_

hydrogen, sulfur, potassium;   oxygen, sodium, iron

305. Write the symbol for each of the following elements:

chlorine _Cl_   zinc _Zn_

calcium _Ca_   carbon _C_

bromine _Br_   magnesium _Mg_

125

Cl, Ca, Br   Zn, C, Mg

306. When an atom gains an electron, it forms an ion with what charge? ___-1___

---

negative

307. The chlorine atom gains one electron to form a chloride ion. The symbol for the chloride ion is ___Cl^-___ .

Cl⁻

308. When two ions are held together by the attraction of their opposite charges, what type of bond is between them? ___ionic___

---

ionic

309. An acid is a substance that yields ___H^+___ ions in solution.

---

hydrogen (or H⁺)

310. A base is a substance that yields ___OH^-___ ions in solution.

126

hydroxide (or OH⁻)

311. Salts yield what types of ions? _any but K⁺ or OH⁻_

---

any ions except H^+ and OH^-

312. A solution that conducts electricity is called _electrolyte_
_____.

---

an electrolyte

313. A solution that does not conduct electricity is called
non-electrolyte.

---

a non-electrolyte

314. Saliva has a pH between 5.5 and 6.9. What type of liquid
is saliva? ____ _weak acid_

---

a weak acid

315. Blood has a pH range of 7.35-7.45. What type of liquid is
blood? _weak base_

a weak base

316. When two atoms share electrons, they are held together by
a ___covalent___ bond.

---

covalent

317. Specific catalysts for living organisms are called
___enzymes___.

---

enzymes

318. Diagram the structure of the hydrocarbon compound containing the following arrangement of carbon atoms, and indicate all the hydrogen atoms.

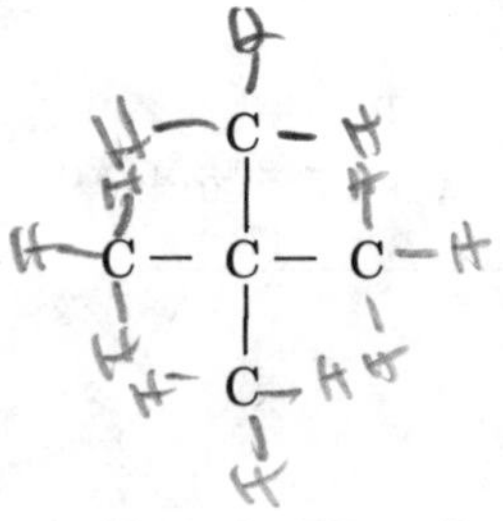

$$
\begin{array}{c}
\text{H} \\
| \\
\text{H}-\text{C}-\text{H} \\
\end{array}
$$

$$
\begin{array}{ccccc}
\text{H} & & | & & \text{H} \\
| & & | & & | \\
\text{H}-\text{C} & —— & \text{C} & —— & \text{C}-\text{H} \\
| & & | & & | \\
\text{H} & & | & & \text{H} \\
\end{array}
$$

$$
\begin{array}{c}
\text{H}-\text{C}-\text{H} \\
| \\
\text{H}
\end{array}
$$

319. Indicate the hydrogen atoms attached to the following arrangement of carbon atoms.

$$
\text{C} \equiv \text{C} - \text{C}-
$$

$$
\text{H} - \text{C} \equiv \text{C} - \underset{\displaystyle \overset{|}{\text{H}}}{\overset{\displaystyle \overset{\text{H}}{|}}{\text{C}}} - \text{H}
$$

320. What is the simplified structure of the compound below?

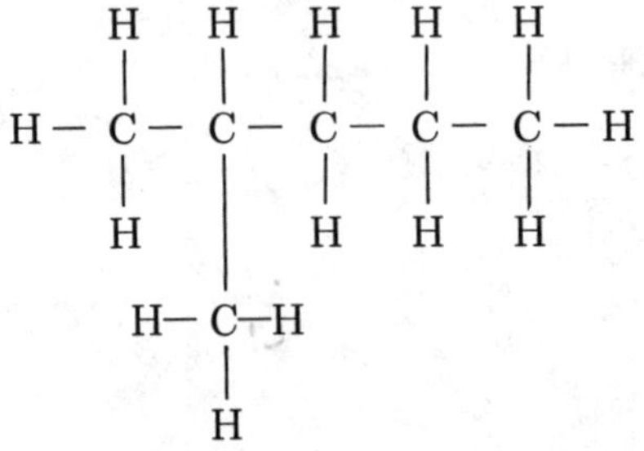

$CH_3CH(CH_3)CH_2CH_2CH_3$

$CH_3CH(CH_3)CH_2CH_2CH_3$

321. What is the simplified structure of this compound?

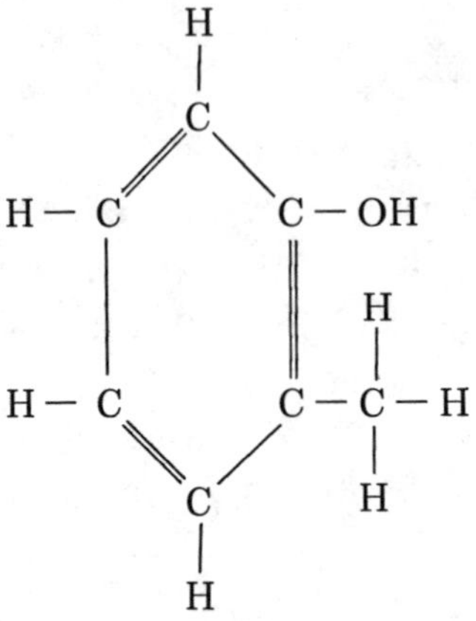

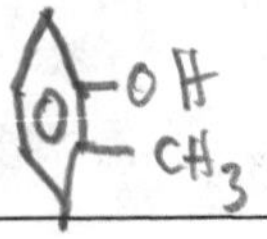

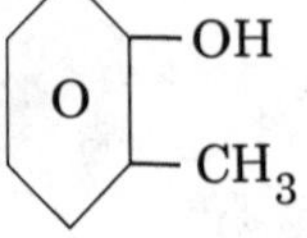

322. What type of functional group is represented by:

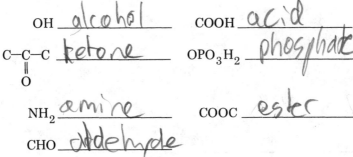

OH _alcohol_   COOH _acid_

C—C—C _ketone_   OPO$_3$H$_2$ _phosphate_
‖
O

NH$_2$ _amine_   COOC _ester_

CHO _aldehyde_

---

alcohol	acid
ketone	phosphate
amine	ester
aldehyde	

323. What types of functional groups are present in each of the following compounds?

NH$_2$

[structure with O and =O on ring]

$$H-\underset{\underset{H}{|}}{\overset{\overset{\displaystyle H}{|}}{\underset{|}{\overset{|}{C}}}} $$

H
|
C = O
|
H — C — OH
|
H — C — OH
|
H — C — OH
|
H — C — OH
|
H

CH$_3$CH(OH)COOH

a. _amine_   b. _alcohol_   c. _alcohol_
   ketone   _aldehyde_   _acid_

a. amine and ketone;   b. aldehyde and alcohols;
c. alcohol and acid

324. Which of the following compounds is a carbohydrate?

a. C_6H_6 (b) $C_{12}H_{22}O_{11}$ c. C_6H_7ON d. C_2H_6O

---

b. $C_{12}H_{22}O_{11}$

325. Hydrolysis of a disaccharide yields ___ 2 monosaccharides_

---

two monosaccharides

326. Starch is a (monosaccharide, disaccharide, polysaccharide) _poly saccharide_.

---

polysaccharide

X *327.* The products of fat hydrolysis are _fatty acids,_ _glycerol_.

---

fatty acids and glycerol

132

328. What functional groups do fats contain? _____acids_____

esters

esters

329. Proteins always contain which elements? _C, H, O, N_

C, H, O, N

330. The hydrolysis of protein yields ___amino acids___.

amino acids

331. The loss of hydrogen is termed ___oxidation___.

oxidation

332. The loss of oxygen is termed ___reduction___.

reduction

333. Indicate whether each of the following reactions involves oxidation or reduction.

a. $CH_3CH(OH)CH_3 \longrightarrow CH_3COCH_3$ _oxidation_

b.

 _oxidation_

c.

$$
\begin{array}{c}
H \\
| \\
C{=}O \\
| \\
H-C-OH \\
| \\
H-C-OH \\
| \\
H
\end{array}
\longrightarrow
\begin{array}{c}
H \\
| \\
H-C-OH \\
| \\
H-C-OH \\
| \\
H-C-OH \\
| \\
H
\end{array}
$$

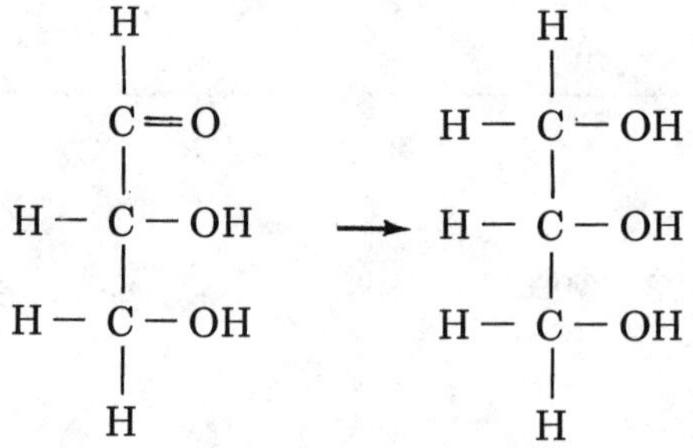

reduction

---

a. oxidation   b. oxidation   c. reduction

Congratulations! You have completed the program. If you have worked conscientiously you should now be able to:

- recognize the elements present in various biological compounds.

- understand the term pH as applied to fluids and cells.

- recognize what is meant by the terms acids, bases, and salts as they occur in plant and animal tissues.

- know what electrolytes are so that their functions in the life of the cell can be more clearly understood.

- understand oxidation and reduction as they occur in the metabolic processes of plants and animals.

- differentiate between carbohydrates, fats, and proteins, and recognize each from its unique functional group.